The Tell All of Camille Jones

A Dallas-Houston Love Triangle

E' Simone

The Tell All of Camille Jones is a work of non-fiction based on real life facts and information. Names, characters, places and incidents are merely the products of the author's imagination or are used fictitiously.

Copyright © 2015 by Empress Hyder
All rights reserved. This book or any portion thereof may not be reproduced or used in any manner whatsoever without the express written permission of the publisher except for the use of brief quotations in a book review.

Printed in the United States of America

First Printing, 2015

For information about special discounts for bulk purchases, please contact Empress Hyder at ehyder1990@gmail.com.

ISBN-13:978-1-5151-0926-6
ISBN-10:1-5151-0926-7

THE TELL ALL OF CAMILLE JONES
A non-fiction novel

Acknowledgements

Never in a million years did I believe I would put my fears aside to live out one of my many dreams of becoming a writer. Putting my own personal mishaps, life lessons and achievements on a platform for the world to see. I was once in a spiritual battle within where I wanted everything to happen overnight. I no longer wanted to remain patient and I had begun to give up, but then one day I realized I was not in control. I had the gift, therefore my job was to solely use my gift in the best way possible and the rest would fall into place. I'm glad I serve an awesome God and was raised by a woman who told me to never let anyone dim my light for the sake of their own insecurities' and shortcomings. It literally took me two long years to put this entire thing together and I made a promise to myself I would never look back once I got started.

Thanks to the most high for blessing with the gift of gab and bluntness. In addition to my determination, wisdom and a foundation that would make this journey worthwhile. Thanks to my first born son, Zyion for giving me a reason to write again. It wasn't until after you spent the longest 37 days of our new life together in NICU when I realized you deserved the best, you deserved my best. The best days are the ones I spend with you knowing you belong to me. For you will carry on my legacy in generations to come.

For reasons more than one, I would like to thank my mother for her unconditional love and support. For always encouraging me to carry out my dreams. For giving me life.

Empress Hyder

Thanks to my siblings for always pushing me to better and protecting me from danger seen and unseen. Thanks to my crew, Tyeese, Tuneshia and Aushia for listening to all my ideas and motivating me every day to go harder than the day before.

Thanks to all of my fallen angels who have continued to watch over me in the darkest hours. Thanks to my mentors Natalie Hambleton and Antoinese Pride, I thank you for taking pride in being an educator and instilling in me the confidence to be great. My favorite Delta Sigma Theta women, you have made such a great impact on my life and I do not know where I would be without the two of you.

Nevertheless, thank you to all of you, my supports and my readers, I appreciate every single one of you. From requesting more, keeping me focused and challenging me to bring my characters to life. Some of you may have not reached the point in your life where you know your purpose, but never give up. On today, I encourage all of you to simply set a goal and create a step by step plan to achieve that goal. Never let anyone and anything stop you from doing the one thing that you love.

Love & Light
E'Simone

Prologue

Empress Hyder

"Abstain from fleshly lusts, which war against the soul."

1 Peter 2:11

Well I'd be damned. Exactly four years later and I'm back in the same situation I prayed myself out of when I was 18 years old. Just like anyone else I've fucked up in the past and I've made mistakes but Lamar would never forgive me if he knew, not only was I still fucking around with Slim, but I'm writing my story, his story, hell our story 5 months pregnant with twins.

In spite of this shortcoming, I've done pretty damn well for myself after graduating from Prairie View A & M University with a Bachelors of Business Administration in Marketing. Might I add with a 3.45 GPA, needless to say, ya girl had it going on.

Not to toot my own horn, but I'm currently a twenty-four year old college graduate, with my own condo in the heart of downtown Dallas, a 2 door Audi A5, which was a graduation gift from Slim unknowingly, and my own marketing firm. All thanks to the money I saved for those rainy days and lonely nights.

Three months ago I founded an organization for teen girls called Project Q.U.E.E.N.S with an overall goal to enhance the mind and broaden the horizon of today's youth. If there was one thing I cared about more than myself, it would be to inform young girls to love themselves first.

Empress Hyder

If I could stop anyone from experiencing the hurt, fear and overall loss of self like what you're about to witness I would tell this story over and over again.

I got and still maintained to get my own everything with the minimum assistance from anyone. And I planned on keeping it that way. Returning home after college was something I just was totally against, but it had to be done so that I could map out my road to success. It was more like a stepping stone than anything. If you ever went away and had to return under the room of an overprotective parent, I'm sure you could relate. Spending four years of your life independent and then having to follow the rules of someone else just did not fly with me. At all. In the meantime I gave myself a deadline, and stacked my chip. I was use to a certain lifestyle and even though my mom was like my best friend, she needed her space and I for sure needed my privacy.

I stopped asking my mother for shit a long time ago. She had done her job; got me through high school, purchased my first car, raised me to be a responsible adult and dropped my ass off at college. So as a favor to her I grew the fuck up with a quickness. There really was no looking back now.

I was young, smart and full of life. Literally nothing could set me back not even God himself. And as a gift of appreciation to my mother, I paid for my graduation pictures, cap and gown and even gave her a poster with my face plastered all over to hang up in her office. Even then, that still would never be enough, because she deserved the world and that's all I ever wanted to give her at the end of the day.

Bitches aimed to be the type of woman I was molding myself to become. Petty hoes hated me and hating hoes admired my stiffness. But I saw no competition. I wanted everyone to do well in life. I would give my enemy the shirt of off my back, if need be, but people weren't raised the way I was raised. The streets were grimy and you had to eat or get ate. But I could definitely hold my own under any pressure. I was who I was for a reason.

In any case though, that all may sound appealing and attractive right?

Conversely, I failed to mention I would soon be sharing not one but two children with a man that already had three bad ass kids he didn't take care of nor did he claim. A man that felt since he was on child support for his oldest son and daughter they were less deserving of his time. He refused to get a real job because in the state of Texas, child support was something they do not play about. Point. Blank. Period. It was coming out of your check, whether your liked it or not. In that aspect he was a nothing ass nigga but under different circumstances he was the man of my dreams and nightmares at the same time. *"I must be one lucky bitch, or a bitch with bad luck,"* were thoughts that would penetrate my mind time and time again.

Like everyone else, I would have never pictured my life would have turned out like this. Let my friends tell it I would marry rich and not want for anything in life. My mother would tell me to not settle for rich and to get my own. Nevertheless, they were close but they missed the part

Empress Hyder

about the lies, cheating and abuse that would come with the territory.

No one could have made me believe I would end up here again. In a place where I felt unappreciated and had been stripped of my self-confidence. I was supposed to be that bitch that no one could break. I was known for breaking hearts and getting what I wanted out of niggas with no feelings involved before meeting Lamar.

I put my life in harm's way, so there was no one to blame but myself. My actions spoke for themselves and the consequences were coming in full effect. Yet, I have no major regrets because once upon a time Slim was exactly what I craved and I was willing to risk it all to maintain my position. Even if that meant going to war with the man I once loved and a bitch I once called my friend. But before you judge me, I'm going to take you back to the very beginning. Take you back to the date, day and time it all started.

Allow me to welcome you to the fucked up world of **MISS CAMILLE NADIA JONES.**

Chapter One

Empress Hyder

"The heart is more deceitful than all else and is desperately sick; who can understand it?

-*Jeremiah 17:9*

◆ ◆ ◆

Let me take you back to almost four years ago. The story unfolds as such; in a day my life changed in the midst of a trap visit in Joppa, Texas and some bomb ass sex. That experience was maybe a once in lifetime chance of having everything I desired. It was now or never to take advantage of all of the material shit that came along with his territory. I mean when you're young, life is about having fun. Life is about finding yourself and making mistakes to get to the lessons you needed to be taught. By no means was not easy to mend the broken pieces to my shattered self-esteem. Many of my relationships and friendships were directly and indirectly affected by my actions. However, at the time I talked myself into thinking it was all worth it. At least that's what I thought.

Everything that glittered was not gold and I damn near paid for it with my life. I promise you I was in for a rude awakening but was blinded by his Lifestyle. Money. Cars. Diamonds.

The grass really wasn't greener on the other side and I would eventually realize it was only green where you watered it. I had confessions to make to myself and until I could face the facts, I would have forever been a lost soul.

For starters I had to admit that there was a serious issue at hand. Secondly, I had to convince myself that I was actually in love with one too many people. Men who were very different, yet had similar backgrounds. Both who

Empress Hyder

cherished me and would go to war behind me and knowing all of this was causing my world to unfold on my journey to self-discovery.

At the age of 20 I separated from my boyfriend of 4 years mentally, sexually and emotionally to be in the arms of a man I barely knew. But no matter what, in my heart, Lamar and I would forever be together. He knew that and every bitch walking Prairie View's campus, from Dallas to Houston knew that. Our relationship had been tested over the years. In more ways that I can explain but the top two killers were the envious females dying to have my spot and the niggas going out of their way to assassinate Lamar's reputation.

I'll admit, at 20, I was a little selfish and careless when it came to love and until this day I still can't put my fingers on what made me that way. It may have been because my father broke my heart before any man had a chance to do so. I remember growing up and wondering if my dad would show up to one award ceremony, birthday party or even a graduation. I still reflect back to all the days I sat out on the porch waiting for his ass to show up and he never did.

"Camille it's not that I don't love you and your brothers, I no longer love your mom."
"So you just make a family and walk out on us, after all the shit we've been through."
"Watch your got damn mouth young lady, I'm still your father."
"Father, I beg to differ you're a sorry ass excuse for a man, some father you are."

One of our last conversations plays over and over again in my mind. And for that I will forever question, who would bring a child into this world and abandon them. I wanted to be a daddy's little girl so bad and he took that from me. I wanted to know what the hell it would feel like to come home and see my dad's face every day. To have a motherfucker really care about your well-being because he made a contribution to your life. Thanks to James, my deadbeat ass father, all of that was ripped from me. He had other shit on his agenda and being a father was not part of it. He had his head so caught up in his new wife's ass after him and my mom split that we only existed when he needed money for commissary.

Not knowing what love was supposed to feel like when it was genuine from a man, I cheated. I cheated on the only man I had been with, for the last four years of my life, to fuck with a dope-boy that had been with everyone. I would soon find out who Slim really was when it was all said and done. Still I kept dusting myself off to try things differently because I thought it was love. But lust had a funny way of disguising itself as such.

What I thought to be love would eventually shine light on every flaw that existed within this Dallas and Houston love triangle. You will never believe how things played out but if you stay engaged you will soon find out.

Slim made me want to leave the one I was with to start a new life with him and I didn't care who didn't like it nor who tried to stop it. I didn't care who was hurt in the process until I realized I was only self-inflicting the hurt on myself.

Empress Hyder

When any man chases you for so long, I'm talking consecutive years, you would've given in too. You probably wouldn't have taken it to the level we reached, maybe you would've entertained him to just find out what he had to offer. We've all been there I'm sure.

Slim would soon be the person to make me feel so high and so low simultaneously. An educated dope-boy that cheated on me with a friend and denied the shit until he got caught in the act. The same "friend" I confided in and cried to with all of my business, and I do mean all of my business. But I suppose that was my bad for letting everybody and their momma know what went on between him and me. We all know those type of bitches, the ones who run their mouths as if they had a point to prove, seeking validation, and signing checks verbally that their asses can't cash. The bitches that swear their pussy had power to make a nigga leave the one they loved. The envious bitches who are really wolves in sheep skin waiting on the right time to catch you off guard.

Yeah, we all know those type of bitches and that's exactly what she was. She played her part for years throughout our college friendship. Oh, but when shit hit the fan, I found out she was the one running back and telling Slim everything. To be honest, I knew she always had been out to get me. I could sense it in the way she would always get curious about what was going on between Slim and I. It was only a matter of time before everything that was done in the dark and between the sheets of our home would come to the light.

I felt like Diamond from the players club and this broad was Ebony, except we weren't related but she played the games just as raw. You would think you had the right to share exclusive information about your relationship with your man with your main female friends, right?

Wrong! Bitches were trifling and I would soon have the facts to back that notion up.

GUESS BYGONES WERE NEVER BYGONES, but back to my story, hell, we will introduce this has-been in the next chapter or so. Definitely not trying to make this duck more popular than she pretended to be. I'm sure she has a story of her own to tell. I'm sure they all have their own version to tell. But this is my tell all and I'm going to carry it out that way until the end.

Loyalty didn't mean shit to her and it was only a matter of time I would begin to find shit out. I guess the saying is true, *"Never share how good the dick is with another woman."* Because while I was being sent out on drops on the other side of town and on trips to get money, to make shit happen for us, this nigga was laid up and pillow-talking with another bitch. Filling this hoe head up with game. Telling us the same fucking thing, as if that shit was cool.

Slim was gassing a female, no fuck that, he was gassing a bitch who would never be me no matter how hard she worked or how hard she tried. And, even she knew that. I remember the text messages vividly from the day I borrowed his car and found an old phone in the middle console. He had her named saved as *"The Spot"*. Which didn't raise a red flag until I noticed the last message was an attachment. And what dope dealer do you know that would send evidence through the phone.

 The Spot- "Hey!"
 Slim- "What's good?"
 The Spot- "Do you want company?"
 Slim- "She's at the crib right now, but fall through in about an hour."
 The Spot- "Ok, I miss you so much"
 Slim- "Lol ma, I miss you too"
 Slim- "aye, I better see that ass in an hour"
 The Spot- "Yes sir, but until then"

And this bitch sent her pussy through a text. But I had no proof it was her. Even though deep down inside of me I knew it was.

 I often asked myself, "how could something so sweet turn bitter when everything thing started out cool?" How could something so great turn so bad, right before my eyes and even I didn't see any of this coming my way. Or maybe I did and I was just in denial and oblivious to the facts.

 I can bet my bottom dollar that was where the problem came from to begin with; everything started out so damn cool, so you know it was destined to go wrong. And it did.

 I found myself doped up, being fucked by niggas I didn't even know and getting my ass whopped numerous times a day for no reason at all. And for the life of me, I still don't understand why I stayed. No matter how many times I called myself getting away and being done. I stayed and put up with his shit for almost two years, just like I stayed and put up with Lamar shit for four years. Now I'm stuck with his ass for life. Or at least for 18 years and then the ultimate decision would be up to the twins in choosing whether or not they wanted to have a relationship with their father. The same choice Ruth gave me when I began to question whether my father loved me or not.

I swear this had to be one of my biggest mistakes, burdens and downfalls. And I've made some fucked up decision throughout life, all incomparable to this one. I knew no one would understand and no one would be extending out forgiveness on the block. My mother and brothers weren't speaking to me at certain points throughout this whole love affair. I only had two friends from back home to call on and I didn't even recognize my own reflection. My mind, body and soul sunk into isolation.

This was the type of shit I read about. Feeling like a trapped prisoner. Where every breath you took, you wondered if it would be your last. This was the type of shit I would see in movies, and my life was becoming exactly that. I was becoming unrecognizable. It was in my actions, in my voice and in the way I carried myself. I had fallen to a point of vulnerability that I wouldn't wish on any woman. All to save face and to keep a nigga out of jail. Then again, let me stop while I'm ahead, because at the rate I'm going, I'll be giving you all of the details and we just met.

So, just sit back, relax, and get as comfortable as you can, because this is about to be the journey to my self-destruction.

Chapter Two

"You're going to come across people in your life who will say all the right words at all the right times. But in the end, it's always their actions you should judge them by. It's actions, not words that matter."

— *Nicholas Sparks, The Rescue*

Empress Hyder

◊ ◊ ◊

His persistence, appearance and charm is what got me. His money and lifestyle is what kept me. The desires of my heart had a great impact of why I put up with Slim for so long.

Growing up in a single parent home I didn't need for anything but I wanted for a lot. My mom had to play the role of both parents but I never seen her grow weary. After my dad left, she fell deep into her spiritual self, whatever the fuck that means. She was saved, sanctified and filled with the Holy Ghost. Don't get it twisted, my mother took a lot of shit, but one thing she didn't tolerate was being disrespected and talking about her kids.

It didn't matter who you were and what you thought you knew, you couldn't tell Ruth shit about her kids. My mother was and still is the epitome of a strong black woman and she would never let her worst enemy starve or see her sweat. She didn't need a man for anything and damn sure was not seeking no man but God.

When I was three years old, she moved my brothers and me to the heart of Pleasant Grove where I would spend the majority of my childhood. We started out on welfare but she didn't allow herself to become dependent of government assistance. I was six years old when she went back to school to get some basic skills underneath her belt before becoming an Administrative Assistant at Sprint. Ruth was a hustler by any means, she didn't have a relationship with her mom growing up but she had this motherhood shit down packed. I think it had something to do with being raised by her step grandmother who had no kids of her own. She literally taught my mom everything she knew except to not let little boys touch your breast.

    Ruth was cut throat and straight to the point because she refused to allow the streets to raise me and my brothers. Gaylen "Dookie" and Napier were my eldest brothers, my only brothers for that matter. Twenty-nine and twenty-seven years of age who ran the streets with some head hunters. I was the runt of the litter and the only girl so I was given nothing but game growing up. No Barbie's. No easy bake ovens. No baby dolls. Game. From knowing how to bleed a nigga dry to knowing how to play the cards that were dealt to me. I was taught you had to be two things in life other than yourself to get what you want. You see Ruth taught me and my brothers how to hustle early, she showed all of us the ropes. She taught me how to walk the walk and talk the talk. She taught me and my brothers to be an ass-kisser when necessary and a bull shitter to get what we wanted when we wanted it. Even if we didn't like the person or the thing, even if we disagreed, we were to get everything we needed out of them before taking it personal. So if I had to "pretend" to like a nigga and sit pretty doing it, I was all down for the foreign exchange.

    Shit, my education at *Prairie View A & M University* was paid for, thanks to my God-given intelligence. I went into college with multiple scholarships. I was proactive in purchasing all of my books and reaching out to all of my professors ahead of time. I was determined to stand out and handle my business so that I could be in and

Empress Hyder

out in exactly four years max. I ended my third semester with a 3.75 GPA and was only four semesters away from graduating, so you know I was feeling some type of way. I couldn't wait to return home to Dallas to put my business plan into play. Time and patience with everything and everybody was the key factor to keeping my composure.

I had come to my breaking point and I needed a break from all the studies and unnecessary bullshit. I knew heading back to Dallas for winter break would give me just that for about a month or so. It was even better that my birthday was a few days away and I was all for being the life of a single-man's party.

Not to mention, I was feeling more like a woman even before I met him. The thought of turning twenty-one had my head so gone, I was already dancing to the beat of my own drums. You couldn't tell me shit. And if you tried to tell me anything I would get dead in your ass at any time and any place.

I was ready to explore the rhythm of hell. I was ready to have some fun and I knew before I engaged in anything it was time for my yearly checkup to make sure nothing snuck up on me. Especially with my history of sexual transmitted diseases that were always a lovely gift from Lamar. Miss kitty and I had to make sure we were in the clear.

Even after everything I was taught over the past twenty plus years even the smartest of us, women, lack better judgment and common sense. Not dumb by a long shot but my street smarts was limited and Slim would soon teach me everything I needed to know about the streets, loyalty and mere survival.

FROM DAY ONE I knew he would be trouble. During one of our late night car rides from 2nd street in South Dallas to the Chick- Fila that sat right off of the service road on northwest highway I promised I wouldn't get caught up. He promised not to let me but everything started happening so fast, my life was slipping out of my hands and dangling at the palms of his.

In a day I was hooked. My soul was being sold. I was caught up in a trance or maybe it was a metaphorical romance. There was something about trouble that excited me. The kind of trouble that you would indulge in just for fun, nothing more and nothing less. The type of trouble that wouldn't hurt anyone. At least I thought.

In a day, one fucking day my life changed drastically. Without my consent. Without any awareness. I was already in too deep and it was only day one.

Rihanna said it best, "Once a good girl goes bad she's gone forever." And I was. Well, maybe, I was only temporarily gone, lost on the dark road of I-45 between Dallas, Prairie View and Houston. Premeditating a self-murder of self by getting involved with Slim.

I met Slim during my winter break in the fall of 2010. An entire month away from the yard, I was relieved and looking for something to keep me occupied. No intentions of that something being someone because I already had a man. Nevertheless, he was in Houston and I was in Dallas and for the last four years this had always been the turning point, yet the breaking point of our relationship.

Empress Hyder

It was a typical Saturday morning at my home in Pleasant Grove. The home I shared with my mother, brothers and nephew occasionally. I was just about finished doing my normal cleaning routine, with my J. Cole station playing on Pandora.

> Miss high profile caught you shopping on Canal
> I guess it makes sense, it seems phony as your style
> Your hair and your nails just as phony as your smile
> Fake eyelashes, you drew your eyebrows
> It make a brother ask, do you pride yourself?
> Your make up like a mask, tryna hide yourself
> It seems on the outside you thinking you the shit
> But there's a soul that's inside that you don't even knew exist
> So you so out of touch that the world mistreat you,
> Rich niggas fuck you and broke niggas beat you

"LOSING MY BALANCE" playing in the background when my phone began to notify me back to back with Facebook and Twitter notifications.

The first time Slim entered my inbox was Tuesday, June 15th, 2010 and there we were in the middle of December and he was at it again. I gave him a hard time for reasons I later forced myself to believe would push away. It was only right to act hard to get. For starters, he was fresh out of jail and I didn't know this man from Abel or Cane.

He would write me multiple times a day and my ol "game playing ass" would simply not reply after a certain point into the conversation as if I were too busy to even lend him a second of my time.

Slim- *"I saw you at 7/11"* was the first message that popped up in my inbox from him.

Me- *"When?"*

Slim- *"Earlier today, lol."*

Knowing he was a damn lie, because I hadn't left my house today and was then I realized this nigga would say anything just to get my attention.

Slim- *"The 7-eleven off of Cockrell Hill in Duncanville."* He added to his previous message.

Me- *"That wasn't me but nice try."*

Slim- *"Oh. My bad"*

Slim- *"I could've sworn that was you."*

Slim- *"So when can I see you?"*

It was then I purposely stopped replying and continued doing what I was doing so I could follow through with whatever plans I had later that night. I often wonder why I did my best to ignore him. He was very attractive and definitely my type. Hell, maybe it was to see if I was worth the chase. Or, maybe it was to see how long he would try before he threw in the towel. Naw, I really think I wanted him but didn't want to seem easy.

Yea, that was it. I didn't want to seem sleazy. I wanted to tease him, because nothing easy is worth keeping, so they say. But hey, can I ask you a question, that's if you don't mind being put on the spot. "Who in the hell are "they" anyway?"

Like who made these rules and set these standards that so many people abide by. Do you and I a favor, when you find out let me know, but in the meantime one thing you will find out about me is that I didn't play by any rules. I found more pleasure in making my own and breaking the ones that were set in stone when it came to being a lady.

Honestly, "Do you feel six months was long enough to make a nigga wait?" Not wait for the pussy but wait in general to even get a number to hit you up every now in then just to make conversation.

There was a reason to my madness. I knew of Slim, but not well enough to entertain him at that moment. If I were going to cheat, whether it be just conversation or a fling, I had the right to at least be picky enough to make sure that someone was worth it. I mean within a day or two of doing my research I found out that hypothetically, Slim was that nigga. The one nigga that made it out the hood and actually went off to college to play ball but fucked around and caught a charge. He was supposed to be locked up for second degree murder but somehow money talks and he walked. Ironically though he caught a charge for a dope case, in which he agreed to serve a thirteen month sentence in the federal penitentiary. Slim had sexed every freak hoe from Dallas to Houston and from Miami to Atlanta. He was an international hoe, but the bitches loved him and his filthy ass draws. Not to mention, Slim had a shitload of baby-momma's to show for it. And without any thinking, second guessing or questioning of his character, intentions, or motives I was selling my soul and risking a relationship already built on the foundation of joy and pain, for a nightmare that would hurt me even while I was awake.

Nevertheless, I only had four semesters left of my undergraduate study. I only had four semesters left to lose myself in the midst of my own self-discovery. I only had four semesters left to walk the same campus with the man who reconstructed my heart, the man I was supposed to marry in spite of all of the times I had been lied to, cheated on and betrayed. That one man that had held me down and had my back through it all, but who in the fuck was I fooling, love didn't pay no bills and that shit definitely gets you hurt. Only the Lord and my journal knows the emotional suffering and discomfort I've been through these past few years.

So now I had only four more semesters left to avoid the hurt I brought upon Lamar. I had four semesters left to make a decision to get out before the world around me began to crumble.

Incidentally, with the devil on my shoulder telling me to do it. To go ahead and see where the conversation with slim would go, reinforcing the fact that I initially had nothing to lose. Consequently, I really had nothing to gain either, being that I am now telling you the story of how my future was brutally altered and destroyed. The story of how I would soon become unrecognizable to myself and everyone around me. But being a person who would generally avoid temptation, I refused to resist it and it would damn near cost me my life.

The messages from Slim were piling up in my inbox, along with over 199 messages awaiting a response and his messages were sitting at the top staring me in my face. I knew I would reply again but in the moment I didn't know what to say or even if this would leave the Facebook world.

It started off with me staring at the screen on my MAC computer, my heart was racing at 100 miles per hour, fingers shaking with trepidation. What I was nervous about, I still have no idea. The following conversation was short, sweet and to the point even though Slim started off running game, as all men around the age of 28 did. Especially when it came to young woman around my age. You could tell by the shit he said he thought I was just some average grove rat that was naïve and unaware of how niggas like him got down. But I wasn't having that shit despite the huge ass age difference. All in all age wasn't anything but a number any way.

I'LL STOP HERE FOR NOW and let me allow you to do some math. Now, if you did your math correctly you will come up with the age difference of 8 years between Slim and I. Slim and Dookie, my eldest brother were neck and neck when it came to age. Dookie could never find out about this shit, reason being he and Slim's younger brother use to be boys back in the day.

So yes, at the time Slim was 8 years older than me, whereas Lamar was one year younger than I was. Just like most fast ass little girls, I've always had a thing for seasoned men, as some like to say. Most of them were experienced, settled and had the majority of life figured out. I use the term "most" loosely, because this experience was a leap to disaster. I had no intentions to crawl before I walked, because I knew for a fact, that even at the tender age of twenty I had heard it all, did it all and seen it all. Perhaps, this would be refreshing or maybe it would refresh my memory as to why I had been with the same dude for 4 years and why I was not as determined to find out.

We would soon exchange numbers and within the first ten minutes of texting back and forth Slim sent me an invite to come over.

"*Camille?*" he texted to make sure he was given the correct number.

Before replying I instantly hopped in the shower and threw on the tightest dress I could find in the middle of the fucking winter. It was a dark fitted blue dressed, with thick multicolored straps, and the back out where the fabric picked up again right above my ass. I accessorized my outfit with my favorite gold watch, some nice gold studded earrings and a cute necklace that dropped into my cleavage with the word "LOVE" attached. Threw on my favorite military thigh high boots and my Euphoria perfume. Niggas love a female that smelled good, so I always kept that in mind.

I just knew he would be calling to tell me to come over and when he did, I didn't want him waiting any longer than he had to.

I rushed into the bathroom to apply some light make-up and lip gloss, and after pulling my Senegalese twist up into a high bun, I returned to the edge of my bed and just waited on his response after letting him know I was on my way. I had to make an impression everywhere I went, I got dressed for him, as I would with Lamar but he was not my man, at least not yet and he already had a hold on me.

Slim- "Give me about five minutes before you come."

Now why the fuck was this nigga playing with my emotions so early on, your guess is better than, what I did want to know was what that mouth did.

Empress Hyder

I just knew he was not already playing games. My number one reason for not fucking with niggas who had kids and baby mommas. I would never come first. Not taking into consideration the type of lifestyle he lived or anything of that nature I immediately begin to assume the worse. Which was typically how females reacted. It was my way or no way and I'd be damned if I would sit around and wait on any nigga looking a fool. Especially one I made wait from the jump. But I found myself waiting.

Really though, "Can you believe I anxiously waited for this nigga out of all niggas to hit me up?" But damn, I needed a nut, therefore I needed to be fucked and he was definitely the person for the job per the rumors. No Quickies. Quickies are not my style. I needed a session where he would take his time but would do it right and just the way I liked it. Thing about this situation was he was someone I had never been with, so I didn't know if he would damage my insides like a nigga fresh out of jail or make love to the depths of my soul. I didn't know anything about Slim outside of what I was told. But I did know that this would not be an innocent visit. I was on a mission and I knew just by the tone of the text we were on the same page and looking for the same thing.

Excuse me for being so blunt, but I'm sure some of you can relate. And if for some strange reason you can't relate, you have probably avoided given in to temptation at the stake of another human being. But don't try to fool yourself, because no one is exempt.

I bet I have you wondering if he asked me to come. Then again, "why wouldn't he want to be in my presence?" I'm a hot commodity as he was, for my own reasons and he was soon to find out why. Hell we both were chasing the same thing in a different direction, with different motives and intentions, but at least we had something in common. We secretly yearned for one another. He desired me and I desired him. After hearing his sex was to die for I made sure to purposely forget to put some panties on for a first-time visit.

BUT LET'S GET TO THE GOOD STUFF. The aftermath. My Story.

I'm going to tell you the entire story in first person, so you can take a walk in my shoes, mentally, physically and emotionally. So you can tell me how you would have reacted in a similar situation. In my eyes, I'm the only person who is aware, other than the other individuals caught up in this love triangle of how it all with down. All the emotions, love, lust and drama that had been thrown around.

So if anybody wants to tell their side of the story because they oppose the way my shit is being told or how they were portrayed, too fucking bad. I'm going to tell it all. I will not sugarcoat anything. I'm not apologizing for putting anyone on blast. I'm Camille Jones, the prettiest, bluntest, and illest motherfucker you've probably ever met.

I WILL BE HEARD. This is all the tea; freshly brewed out the kettle. Even then you still will not know the half of it but stay tuned because you all are in for some first-class love triangle, back stabbing, and hood chronicle shit. I had never encountered anything as intense and grimy as what

Empress Hyder

you're about to continue witnessing. No man or woman was safe when lust came into the picture. Love was only something we all desired and had no idea we were being fooled.

    It's never too late to justify your mistakes and use them as lessons instead of failures. Subconsciously I found myself trying to please everyone I ran into who were afraid to play dress up in their skeletons. So many people had so many unrequested ass opinions about how this story should be told. Then when we all were at the end of the ropes about who would tell their side first, I realized then I was already better than them. Everything about this situation happened exactly how it was supposed to happen and now I have a story to tell. So bear with me as the truth, my truth unfolds right before your eyes.

Chapter Three

Empress Hyder

"Love, like everything else in life, should be a discovery, an adventure, and like most adventures, you don't know you're having one until you're right in the middle of it."

— *E.A. Bucchianeri*

◈ ◈ ◈

I decided to roll me up two mini Swisha Sweets filled with the best exotic Kush you could find in the states. I poured me a glass of Hennessy knowing I had to at least get my mind right and distract myself from all the lusting and sinning I was about to partake in.

I had these vivid, impure images of me and Slim replaying over in my head. The more I started to picture him deep stroking his manhood between my legs the more anxious I became.

My mind was racing so damn fast, on some I know this nigga didn't just get my number to not use it. I was ready to see what the hype was about. I almost siked myself out and shit. Hell, but one hit of that Kush between my manicured nails, and it was straight fuck it mode.

Waiting was for the birds and I was about to make some other moves but then there it was, in big bold letters,

Slim- "*WYA?*" followed by a "come thru." You should have been there to witness how fast I jumped at his demand. I grabbed all of my shit in about five seconds flat; my stash, my bottle, my clutch, my keys and some panties and headed downstairs to the car.

THAT FIVE MINUTES DOWN THE ROAD FELT LIKE FOREVER, but I think my conscience start trying to kick in or some shit and I wasn't for it. I had never looked at another man other than Lamar yet alone been fucked or touched by another man. So, I began to question myself.

"Was I really going through with this?"

"Should I turn around?" All the damn questions I didn't want to answer, began to surface. It was already too late. I was already parked in front of one out of several of Slim's trap houses somewhere in Joppa, Texas waiting for this nigga to come outside and invite me in.

The front door swung of this run down shack opened and I instantly began taking shots of hen to the head, about 4 in a matter of 60 seconds. I didn't want to remember any of this shit. I needed to be in my zone and there was no doubt about that. Especially if I was going to risk losing Lamar over some overhyped peen. By the time I swallowed my last shot, Slim was outside my door in nothing but his Jordan sweats, some 12's with no shirt.

My eyes were glued and gazing at the body of this man. He never said a word, but he had a smile that had me wanting to drop to my knees and please him in a way I knew he had never been pleased before. However he didn't quite have it like that. At least not yet!

"You getting out?" he asked as if I came over to sit in the fucking car.

"If you move, I can." I replied sarcastically.

"Dang I just got here and you're already sweating me." I whispered and we both began to laugh in unison.

I guess he wanted to be a gentleman or some shit like that, opening my door like I couldn't let myself out. I stumbled out the car and fell into his arm. These strong sexual desires started to violate my concentration. On the other hand, the way he hugged my body with his hands in the crease of my waist brought back evocative images of Lamar.

"Why in the hell would his face pop up into my head repetitively?" as if he knew I was about to indulge in some shit I would grow to regret. I put my phone on silent to stop it from buzzing, ringing, and vibrating. I had voice-mails, text messages, and missed calls from Lamar.

Lamar- "Baby?"
Lamar- "I know you see me calling you."
Lamar- "Hello."
Me: "I'm talking to momma give me a second."

I had to come up with a lie and it had to be hasty, in order to make Lamar feel comfortable enough to know everything was fine and I would hit him back later when I found the time.

Seconds into my visit, I stepped into the bathroom to return Lamar's phone calls. But of course he wanted to play the phone-tagging game. He knew from experience I would only call him once and text twice and that was it. Hell if he wanted to talk, we would. Then again we rarely talked anyway, despite the fact he has no phone conversation, we stayed busy, and texting was convenient. Nonetheless hanging out in the bathroom of a trap house wasn't an option.

"Are you ok in the there?" I could hear Slim asking from the living room, which sat directly across from the bathroom.

"I'll be out in a second." I responded over the noise from flushing the toilet to make it seem as if I had really gone to the bathroom. It was almost as if Lamar had perfect timing. As soon as I put one hand on the door to exit, my phone began to vibrate. I couldn't turn around and go back into the bathroom, which would have been too obvious. But Slim was not my nigga either so I had nothing to hide.

"Hello."

"Why are you whispering?" Lamar asked.

"I'm not, but what's up." I replied swiftly.

"You tell me, you sound like you're busy." He responded before carrying on a continuous conversation with whomever he was around.

The conversation lasted no more than five minutes tops, and after a few "I love You's" and a few giggles, I was in the clear. Making me smile when we weren't arguing was one thing he was good at. He knew ignoring me was a no go for me so I hung up the phone all while Slim watched in silent. I truly believe up until this day that was all the ammunition he needed to make his next move.

Before I could even remove the phone from my ear, it was being taken out of my hands for them to be placed on the wall and kisses from the softest lips I've ever felt in life began to trickle down my spine.

I was trying to change my mind attempting to find happy thoughts of Lamar. I was searching deep for memories to escape this thrill. For the life of me and for the sake of my relationship I didn't want it to feel right. But it did. For some reason it did.

Chapter Four

Empress Hyder

"For anything worth having one must pay the price; and the price is always work, patience, love, self-sacrifice."

– *John Burroughs*

◊ ◊ ◊

Slim and Lamar were opposites by a long shot, but similar in some areas of life. For starters, Slim's government name was Ethan J. Watkins.

When I first found that shit out I thought to myself, *"How in the hell did he get a white boy ass name like Ethan."* The name was simply not cute. However, the only two people I could blame in their absence were his sorry ass parents. Slim was a foster kid, his mother fled town to get away from his abusive father who was addicted to drugs. His father eventually died of an overdose leaving him in the care of his aunt who died of full blown AIDS. Three months after her burial, Texas Child Protective Service placed him in their system at the tender age of 6. So Slim, well Ethan, still had a lot of anger built up and if I was good at something it was caring. I probably cared a little too much, but it just wouldn't stop even in the middle of the chaos.

By the time he got to high school; drugs, fighting and money was all that he knew, but his heart, was in the game of Football. He walked on during his first semester at Florida A & M University and it pretty much ended there. I guess college really isn't for everybody and he gave up his college dream for the lifestyle he had once escaped. It was all the he was accustomed to so could you really blame him. Slim was filled with potential all around. The potential to go pro, to be a great father, an admirable companion and the epitome of a man with a plan.

Empress Hyder

He was a combination between Desmond "Dez" Bryant and Calvin Johnson when it came to being the best receiver in college football, but after receiving news his first child would be born he returned back to Dallas in attempt to be a family man. That landed him back in the streets of the Greedy Grove for the fucked up life he once left behind.

His skin was honey brown. A hazel-eyed devil he was. Puerto Rican and African American, he stood at six foot five and two hundred-fifth teen pounds all man with something 10 inches thick in his pants. He had dreams and wishes to make it out the hood but that ship has sailed afloat.

And here I was, a faithful schoolgirl, who had cleaned up my act; always wanting to change the world and a sucker for sob stories, I was being reeled in. I guess that's why I stayed and played the part. Not realizing that someone would end up hurt.

We were oil and water. We didn't mix anything but sex juices and sweat, and that was enough. No matter what though, He would never be Lamar.

Lamar J. Tatum, was every woman's dream. His handsome ass was exactly that from his head to his feet. He was six foot four and one hundred and eighty five pounds of greatness and this man, my man was going places. He was bowlegged and talked real fast, but he was definitely eye candy.

He signed with the Houston Texans and would be starting following graduation. As an agriculture major and the star quarterback of the Prairie View A & M University football team, I had my hands full and together we were ideally a power couple. Nobody wanted to see us together.

They would question how we got together, and instead of rooting for us they were trying to tear us apart.

We were two individuals with a past that should have kept us from even wanting to get to know each other but it only brought us closer. I was his yellow bone eerie beauty. My beauty couldn't help but add to my mystery, which is why Slim desired to get his hands on something that belonged to another man.

I met Lamar when I was 16 years old at a house party during one of my family's random trip to Houston. As soon as I stepped into the living room where the music was rocking the walls, everyone stared in silenced, awed by my burgundy curly natural Afro, my full lips, plump nose, 34d breast, and ass that sat so right in my favorite pair of Levi shorts. As I carried myself, tall and slender, gracefully and elegantly towards one of the men in the room. I felt like a queen, high and regal, with a strange air of mystery behind my cocky smirk. Although my almond shape eyes were set a little far apart, I was, even with the flaws, and all the tattoos that added to my complex, one of the most beautiful women he had ever seen. I could tell by the gaze in his eyes he just couldn't help to think, what kind of woman I was.

So that's why, when I floated out the room moments later, he followed me. He followed me, that man of mine. I get wet just thinking about it, and as the juices began to flow down my thighs, I realized, those were just memories.

Memories that played through my head, over and over again like a broken record. I was a burning candle on both ends. At this instance, my life was one moment of insight after another.

Empress Hyder

The cold hand that gripped my warm flesh, instantly brought me back to reality. The reality of me being led into the door of a bedroom filled with nothing but the nicest furniture and a layout I knew for sure he hadn't designed.

On the inside I was panicking, because I wasn't sure if I was ready to dive into this shit head first. I wasn't sure if I wanted anything to do with this. Yet, that was before I was picked up by the waist and pinned to the only accented wall in his bedroom. The wall supported my back and his shoulders supported my legs.

I was caught off guard when a feeling of warmth shot across my clit. He had two fingers inside of me, another hand grabbing my nipple, and was doing this trick where he held and sucked my clit with his lips while using his tongue to lick my clit at the same time.

Slim had a tongue so moist, the uncontrollable moans drowned out all of the memories of Lamar. I had come to the realization that there had possibly been something missing in my life these past four years. From that moment forward, I realized by the end of the night I would not be done with this fling we had just jump-started. The lustful gaze in his eyes gave me the impression that neither was he.

From the wall, to the floor and finally to the bed. From my hair follicles to my toenails I was being pleasured for sure while getting thrown all around that damn room.

This man had a lot of stamina and was murdering my insides. By no surprise to man, I was loving every second of his rock hard dick inside of me. But being I have a high tolerance for pain, so you know I wanted to feel every inch of what he had to offer.

I WAS SO CAUGHT UP IN THE MOMENT, I hadn't realized that Slim had hit me with the okie-doke and never put on a rubber, but I was too far into this shit to make a big deal out of it. Plus, our flesh pushing up against one another, and the essences from my climax dripping down onto the sheets as I clung to him had me not wanting to ruin this moment.

"Welcome to my world ma." He whispered in my ear. Unsure of how to respond, I instantly leaned back and relaxed on his pillow top California king mattress and gazed at the ceiling. From his actions you could tell that he was not new to this. He knew exactly what he was doing and why he was doing it.

"When I'm done, you will be mine". Slim spoke softly with a straight face. Not one smirk. Not a smile. Nothing.

"Yeah, right. Whatever, handsome." I tried to say without a smile on my face.

I'm sure it was a thrill for him to be playing around in another nigga's pussy. I mean that was my motivation for fucking another bitch man when I was younger, but we won't discuss that.

He knew exactly how to take my mind off of the fact that I would feel guilty later, I mean that's because I was human and my conscience was well intact.

Ethan, at this point I had to call him that, had me feeling like the only bitch in the world. I was becoming confused because I've been fucking since I was 12 so it couldn't be the sex. Maybe I was blowing this shit out of proportion. Maybe just maybe this was some temporary,

Empress Hyder

spare of the moment shit. However, I had to be losing my mind to be giving up a man that was every woman's dream for a hood nigga that was every "bad bitch" fling.

For about 4 minutes we laid there. Our bodies drenched in sweat, him on top of me, we just laid there. But an idle mind is the devils playground and for once in my life I didn't want to think about anything but nutting on his dick. Ready to release all of that pressure I had built up.

Can you believe that nigga had just allowed his dick to lay inside of me, like I was on birth control or something?

Little did he know I stopped taking my birth control pills months ago when I got pregnant by Lamar the second time, but that situation is another story.

At the time I was one abortion down and would do it again if I had to. I was 20 years old and kids were not in my plan, call me a murderer or whatever but shit I was young and still trying to have fun and I just simply wasn't ready.

Despite all the damn commotion coming from outside in that infested ass neighborhood I was giving up my jewels in, he decided he wasn't through with me just yet.

With one hand around my neck, he slid his other hand down the inside of my thigh sending nothing but chills through my entire body.

I laid there, with a limp physique, so exhausted from all of those climaxes I had just experienced in the past 45 minutes. I had no energy whatsoever to stop him. No energy to even pull myself from where I laid to make a clear exit.

There was absolutely no room to breathe and no room to think. But for sure that was what my body needed.

Once again, I allowed my legs to grant him access to my silky pussy as he slide his fingers in and out before slowly inserting himself back into me. I let out a loud moan as he rubbed his palm over my clit in small circles.

I didn't have any more to give, shit honestly I had nothing to give in the beginning because I didn't even belong to myself. I pressed my face against his shoulder and whispered in a soft and helpless tone, "Slim, I can't take this anymore."

The mischievous look in his eyes let me know at that moment, I gave him the power he had been seeking since the moment I stepped through his front door. He wanted me to want him. He wanted me to need him, and without any warning he shoved his dick even deeper inside of me making sure he made all 10 inches count. He toyed with my G-spot and my legs began to shake uncontrollably.

"I'm about to fucking cum." I moaned trying to control the volume of my voice.

"Shit, I am about to cum." I cried out gripping the right side of the mattress,

"Baby, please, please stop." I whimpered.

I could tell that shit turned him on more the sex itself. He began to fuck me faster and even more senseless. He brought his body closer to mine, wrapped his arms around my legs and began to penetrate my walls as deep as he could go. I was losing control of myself, and he was gaining full control of my body, mind and soul.

I grabbed him by the back his head and kissed him hungrily. I swear I felt my soul surrender. I was dancing with the devil. He didn't want me to move an inch. So he positioned me how he wanted me. In the back of my mind all I could think was, this shit would take some getting used to.

"Come here", he said in my ear.

Everything about his voice made my pussy overflow with bodily liquids. My mouth began to kiss every inch of his body, from his chest up to his ear, and I hit the jackpot. His ear out of all the parts on the human body made his flesh weak and tender. It had to be something because his dick sprang to instant attention and finally, finally there were nothing but grunts and moans from a nigga who just, five seconds ago, had my ass under a sex spell with his toxic love potion.

Without any hesitation I tighten this glorious pussy of mine, squeezing his ten inch demon that lay inside of me. At that very moment, of what felt like he was buried inside of my forbidden fruit, gasping for breath, he picked his solid ass up off of me. His eyes drifted closed and his mouth opened wide, finally my mission was accomplished. Or maybe it had just begun.

Being who I was I couldn't let this nigga think he could just fuck me and go to sleep. So I decided to let him regroup for about ten to fifteen minutes. I was still horny, and I needed this shit to last me until I got back to Lamar.

It was my time for sure. I realized the only position we hadn't done was the cowgirl. My all-time favorite. Riding dick was my specialty, my fatality, and my finisher. And if anyone of us were going to leave there with some bragging rights, it sure in the hell was not going to be him. I woke this nigga up with a mouth so slippery wet, you wouldn't have thought I had teeth. I kissed him from his neck down to the shaft of his piece, got it just wet enough for me to pull myself on top of him and have my way. His eyes began to open, his right hand cupped my breast while his left hand gripped my ass. Before I knew it, my ass was being slapped, my hair was being grabbed, our bodies were jerking in different directions and it was over. After 3 plus hours of nonstop lusting and meaningless fucking, it was over.

    All I wanted was a shower and some food to satisfy my appetite after satisfying my flesh.

    I got dressed within seconds, gathered my things and headed to the door. Before I could even get my ass fully into the living room, he asked me to sit next to him. I didn't know what to expect at this point, being that, minus the sexual attraction we were complete strangers to one another.

    "We need to talk", he said, in a very cautionary tone.

    At this point I was so fucking confused because I didn't know this nigga well enough to have anything to talk about. I was all around nervous and scared shit-less.

    I've heard too many stories about the bitches he had beat down and fought on, and I was not about to be anyone's victim. It was getting late and I had to get home, but to be in the presence of a man, when you're man doesn't give you all the attention you demand, was exactly what I needed. I was lonely hell and nobody likes to be lonely, so I did what I needed to do for Camille and trust, I didn't give a fuck how anyone felt.

    Because Lamar was far from a saint. He was every woman's dream for a reason. But I don't think any of you are ready for all of that. I promise you there was more than one

Empress Hyder

reason to why this shit was going down the way it was. And the more I began to think about all the other bitches I've been humiliated in front of, I felt it was only right to give Lamar a dose of his own medicine.

"Why?" I questioned. Hoping this conversation wouldn't las long. I had to find a way to escape without him feeling used and before I could even reach for my phone, I was saved by a call from my girl Renay Blackman.

RENAY BLACKMAN was your typical innocent country girl from Lubbock, Texas but I saw right through that shit. We met during our freshman year floor meeting in the University Commons in the fall of 2009. Building 47. She lived on the 1st floor and I lived on the second. We both had a closest full of skeletons, but through the drama, lies and pain we remained friends. A year long friendship felt like a lifestyle because she had nothing but my best interest at heart since day one. So you could see, why she would be the one to randomly pop up on my caller id. I was almost certain she knew I had gotten myself in some shit that only she could talk me through. We had this weird ass connection with one another. We sensed when something was wrong. We knew when things were all good. We kept in touch. But even as close as we were, I didn't trust her.

While grabbing my keys off the table, Slim began to caress my ass, knowing I was getting ready to head out.

"Hold on girl." I said balancing the phone between my ear and my shoulder. With no words at all Slim walked out the door and to my car.

"I guess I'll see you sooner than later." There was a pause before he began to suck the bottom of my lip. I hesitated to leave. You know how it is. Not wanting to leave, but having to leave to handle business. Yes. That feeling.

"Hey girl," she screamed from the other end of the phone.

"What's going on ladybug?"
She giggled and replied, "Nothing much, just checking on ya."

"How's Dallas?" she asked.
With no warning, I gave her the scoop on Slim, because I'm definitely a tell it all kind of person. She was aware of the messages when they first started but had been in the blind since then. I told her how it went down and what went down, shit the conversation got so good I didn't realize I had already made it to the house.

So, I decided to continue talking on the phone in my car, because I refused to walk into the house where my eavesdropping ass family laid their heads.

We came to the conclusion I was damned if I did and damned if I didn't.

Chapter Five

"The man who does not value himself, cannot value anything or anyone."

— *Ayn Rand*

Empress Hyder

◆ ◆ ◆

I struggled getting in the house because burglar bars were the only way to stop your shit from getting stolen in the Grove. Hell sometimes that wasn't even enough to keep the crooks away but luckily the neighborhood watch LuLu wasn't letting anything go down on our block.

    I crept up the stairs, as if I were a thief in the night to avoid waking my mom who lay asleep in her room directly across the hall from me. I made it in my room, making sure not to shut the door too hard. Closed the door behind me and slid down the wall in disgust at the fact that I smelt like another man.

    I began to undress myself as if he was watching, and suddenly heard some movement outside my door. My mom was slicker than oil, and crept around like a mouse. She was always into shit, because her insomnia kept her up at night. I dived into my bed with a quickness, pulling my zebra sheets over my head, pretending to be sleep before whoever came into my room.

    As soon as I exhaled, there was my mom, peeping her head through the door asking every question in the damn book, as if that shit could not wait until the morning.

    "What time did you get home?" She asked.

    "Did you set the alarm?" She barked.

    "Did you put the food up?" She continued with all these damn questions

"Yes Ma," I responded with a sense of irritation in voice. Followed by a few, yes and no's, to hurry up and send her on her way.

I mean, I guess she was only doing what mothers do. Or her ass was up waiting for me to get home to see if I was actually coming home. Shit was different being back at home for the duration of my winter break. Usually she was a tad bit more relaxed but this time she had become worrisome.

She ended her nightly visit with a kiss on the cheek and said some shit that has stuck with me until this day. With a sense of worry in her eyes, knowing I was living a lie, in the sternest voice she whispered through the cracks of my door as she pulled it ajar, "Don't you go changing on me."

"What the entire fuck did she know?" I asked myself.

Never mind that question. "*Why the entire fuck did she say what she said?*"

The feeling of disappoint shot through my veins. My mother had the same look in her eyes she had the first time I came home with two big ass burgundy hickies on my neck at the tender age of 14. Little did she know that was my first time experiencing anal sex with some random guy around the corner, only because I was on my period.

To her knowledge I was pure. I honestly felt, she never put anything past me. But to her I was her innocent little girl, the only girl she carried out of three children. I was the princess of the flock and my mother wouldn't believe anything about me, even if it came from Jesus himself.

Empress Hyder

"Moment of honesty
Someone's gotta take the lead tonight"
Decline...
"Moment of honesty
Someone's gotta take the lead tonight"
Decline.

Answering my phone was not on my agenda for the night and he could call my phone a million times and every time I would decline.

At this point, I didn't give a damn if I talked to Lamar or not. Hell, it wasn't like he called, texted or was waiting on me to hit him up. We had a dysfunctional ass relationship. The only nigga in the world I know that could run his mouth all day but when it came to me he had nothing to talk about.

Knowing him, he was probably out and about with these random ass friends he finds every other day. So in attempt to forget about everything I decided to take a soothing bubble bath to soak in the mess I created.

Everything and I do mean everything became so relaxed but nothing made sense. I just wanted to shut my mind down and start over. If it was that easy for me to freely give myself to another man why in the fuck was I still worrying about hurting Lamar?

"You want to know why?" Shit here it goes!!!!

Lamar owed me everything in his possession. Even his fucking life. And I would make for damn sure, I was going to be the only female reaping benefits even though I've never been his only one. So I was all in. I wanted my cake and wanted to eat it too. I wanted to be even, even though two wrongs didn't make a right. I was 1 to 10 that I knew of, so this really counted for nothing. *"Or did it?"*

Awaken by a phone call from Lamar I just let the melody of our favorite song play out.

*"Moment of honesty
Someone's gotta take the lead tonight
Whose it gonna be?
I'm gonna sit right here
And tell you all that comes to me
If you have something to say
You should say it right now
(Drake: You should say it right now)"*

I had exactly three weeks left in Dallas and I wanted to spend the remainder of the time I had left with Slim. That's if he allowed me to.

THE NEXT MORNING, when I arose from sleeping like a drunken toddler, I had the biggest hangover. I wanted to throw up everything I was keeping balled up inside of me. My legs were weak. Body tense. Head throbbing. Despite the temporary sickness, I managed to send out my morning motivational messages as scheduled, followed by a simple good morning to his inbox and in return I received an error message.

"What the fuck?" was all that came to my mind.

I immediately went into a panic, maybe he had gotten what he wanted and dipped. I was becoming fucking hysterical, and needed someone to talk to in attempt to calm myself, so you know who I called.

The one and only Lamar!

Empress Hyder

He got me to the point where I could inhale and exhale. At least that was something he was good at even after all of these years of distress. He got me so relaxed I almost slipped up and addressed him by another man's name.

He had no idea what was going on and if he would have asked I probably would have told him. I would have told him everything, for the reason that I know we were just holding on to hope.

Eventually I sent another text to Slim explaining to him that maybe I deserved the cold shoulder. His instant reply let me know I was on his mind too. He asked me to explain what I was talking about and I could almost see the expression on his face, clear as day, with his phone in his right hand as he slouched on his brown love seat while replying. Once again, without any sureness and as requested, I further explained that I had underestimated him and he consoled me with a two wrongs don't make it right, maybe there was hope, and maybe my nightmare was ending and a dream was beginning.

In reality, I wish I could have mixed and matched the two of them to make the perfect nigga.

"Sounds crazy right?"

I actually had someone tell me that once when he cheated on me because supposedly his side piece was everything I wasn't. He told me, me and her together made the perfect woman for him. I was 13 years old at the time, far from a woman, nevertheless he was only 15 years of age going on 16. *"What the fuck did he know about being with a fucking woman anyway?"*

But to hell with all of that. It made no sense then, but at this point I was trying to find all kinds of excuses to make this shit feel right and acceptable.

I was in the valley all by myself trying to find my own way through the darkness without being blinded by love as free spirit seeking power through lust. At least it was with a nigga he didn't know verses the ex-boyfriend he took me from.

The temptation felt like quicksand, I was becoming addicted to his kryptonite during the coldest winter ever.

My last three weeks in Dallas felt equivalent to the 4 years I had been with Lamar. Emotions were at an all-time high. Visits began to happen more frequently. Lies began to create themselves. And in the midst of it all I was two Zithromax pills away from clearing up the fucking Chlamydia I contracted from Slim.

Luckily, whether it was their luck or mine, a trip to the doctor cleared all that shit up. The last thing I needed was to get back to PV knowing I've cheated and pass an infection to the man who I claimed to be faithful to. I guess my pussy was not loyal after all. At least not NOW. It's fucked up when you think about.

I felt like my world was turning. I was moving in circles. The three of us were playing the circle game and eventually I would be left to choose who to walk away from and who to walk away with.

If I would have taken a gift from Slim and gave it to Lamar we would almost be even. I can't count on my hands how many times I've sat in a damn doctor office because of Lamar. So to be pregnant with twins despite it being by

Empress Hyder

another nigga is merely a blessing. I swear my ass was infertile. I swear that abortion I had at the request of Lamar fucked up my insides. I swear on a lot of shit but I guess my life was taking control of itself.

    As a woman though, there are just some things you need to know about yourself, your pussy, and everything else that belongs to you and it's as simple as not granting everybody access to your shit. That last sentence is exactly what made it so easy to slide right through the cracks of my broken relationship. Lamar was slacking and left the doors open for another man to creep in.

    I needed some healing, reassuring and Slim, even if it was temporary. I was growing tired of the redundant arguments. I had no more tears to cry and I no longer had the strength to yell until I was blue in the face. I no longer could put forth the effort for both parties involved in our relationship.

    The truth of the matter is, Lamar was selfish, cocky, and arrogant. Knowing him, he probably wouldn't have even been affected by this shit if he found out anyway. He had his mind made up, that no matter what, I would be his.

    True enough, maybe I was to blame for him feeling that way, because I always second guessed moving around when he would be out doing his thing.

    But maybe times were changing. Perchance our love had run its course or perhaps this was a phase for him to see that someone else out there could and had intentions to reap the benefits of having me.

    Lamar was egocentric in all that he did. And because my selfless ass loved my man, I put up with all of his shit. "Can you believe, one day I had to give him an ultimatum and on that day we would either make it or break it?" We would either be angry in love or at peace as friends.

Of course, like most niggas he took me for a joke because every time I threatened to leave, I could never gather up the courage to do so. The thought of having to start over from scratch and having to tell another man all my deepest secrets, meeting the family, blah, blah, blah, shit I just didn't have time for, scared the hell out of me.

On that day, we talked on the phone for almost two hours in attempt to come up with any possible solutions to get me and him on the same page. For once we were trying to work together, which was some shit we never did.

On the other hand, before I returned back to Prairie View, to tackle another semester, I meant business, and if it meant being single, then I just would have walked away empty handed.

I always questioned if I was good enough to be by Lamar's side or not. Like was I the woman created for him. "Were we destined to be together or were we forcing it?" I constantly wondered was I "too much" woman for him. Because there would be times when he never knew what to say to cheer me up, how to react, yet along act as a boyfriend. In my honesty opinion, those are some things I feel should've come second nature to a man when being in a relationship.

"So who do you blame?" Me. Him. Or the bum bitches he had been with before me.

From what I had witnessed they didn't require much time and effort, they were just happy to be kept, but this

Empress Hyder

time around I was doing the keeping. After all those years, I needed him to realize shit was different now, especially dating someone like me. I was seeking mutuality, respect, commitment, dedication, growth, and longevity.

But, I could see how Lamar struggled with such adaptation, as I was all about accepting challenges with open arms, knowing he would be a challenge. In reality, a man can't give a woman his all if he's unhappy with himself and/or his circumstances.

Those circumstances were exactly what Lamar was dealing with back at home. His mother suffered from lupus, so oftentimes she would have these medical episodes causing us to have to fly to Houston in the middle of many nights to make sure she was ok. He was her only child and she was all he had. Their bond was unbreakable, consequently through it all I was right by his side and even that wasn't good enough. Reason being that there were plenty of times he would borrow my car and use his mom as excuse to fuck around with his ex-girlfriend back at home.

Our biggest problem was consistency. Hell at this point, I was beginning to feel all niggas were the same. They would start some shit, get comfortable, and leave your ass high and dry crawling back to drawing board.

Maintaining a relationship is a damn job within itself. I think motherfuckers forget that all the time and money you put into someone is an investment. Ironically, Slim felt I was worth every silver dollar to his name. He had it in his mind that he would repay me for all the suffering ever caused to me at the hands of another man.

Though my days in Dallas were limited Slim put forth all the time and effort. He took advantage of the time remaining even after I got in his ass about keeping his dick in check. Just thinking about it, pisses me off because that was some nasty shit. I promised my gynecologist she would never see me again, but yet again my ass ended up in a waiting room, bored as fuck, being starred at by some damn Mexicans, waiting for my name to be called.
   I guess it was the price I had to pay for stepping out on Lamar, but at this point and at the expense of my agony I was prepared to get everything I could get out of this nigga.

Chapter Six

"Everything that happens to you is a reflection of what you believe about yourself. We cannot outperform our level of self-esteem. We cannot draw to ourselves more than we think we are worth."

— *Iyanla Vanzant*

Empress Hyder

◆ ◆ ◆

Cheating started to become so easy being that I was partially emotionally detached from Lamar. There were days he would go without calling me, disrespecting our relationship by staying out until five o'clock in the morning and never apologized for the way he made me feel.

Here we were, four years and some change and Lamar still didn't get it. The same way he found time to do everything else was the same fucking effort I deserved in my god damn relationship. Four years I put everything I had and everything I owned into a man who never gave me the credit for even loving his ass wholeheartedly. It seemed as if most men fail to realize that you have to do your part before someone else does it for you.

Giving into the temptation at the hands of any nigga became intentional. I was at the point where everything was fair game. I was hurting and if I wasn't getting the attention from my man it had to come from somewhere.

There were so many downfalls in our relationship, and they were coming my way full speed. For starters, I was the only one out of the two of us with a car and he made every excuse he could pull out his ass to never come to Dallas. Not even on my dime. So instead of the continuous weeping, pleading, and cries out for time, appreciation, and love, I was in this relationship because it was familiar. The thrill left months ago.

Lamar was my comfort zone, and I was settling for momentary happiness. I had all my joy bottled up in one man, so he had the power to control my mood on most days. I would soon come to the realization that I was becoming cold-hearted by the second. I knew, if there was one thing that would get under his skin, it would be me acting as if I didn't care. Being nonchalant with Lamar was his biggest fear above all and the only person to blame would be himself.

I was doing everything to get his attention. I would text him multiple times in an hour. I would offer to come visit. I would call in attempt to hear his voice. I would text him good morning because I was always the first to. I carried out the duties as any real girlfriend would.

To hell with that distance makes the heart grow fonder shit, because that alone had my mind wondering. The more I began to wonder about what he was doing, knowing what he was capable of, the easier it became for Slim.

Right before the semester ended I was out of town for a graduation party with my business organization and when I returned Lamar was acting stranger than usually. On this particular night he barely spoke and would beat me to sleep from that night forward. He would never face me in the shower, and this went on for about three or four days. I knew then his ass was guilty of something especially when the behavior became consistent. Everything about it raised a red flag. We hadn't fucked in days. He skipped out without giving me my morning kisses and he knew I didn't play about those. With his actions he was really putting whatever it was

Empress Hyder

in my hands but I was at a point to where I no longer cared to address it. That wasn't until I logged into my twitter account and a bitch I didn't even socialize with asked had I talk to Lamar. She even had the nerve to ask me if he and I were still together and that's when it became a problem. Obviously this was bigger than what it was and it was time to get to the bottom of it. I was about to lose my cool but before I allowed anyone to see me in that state, I waited until he came home one night after practice. He was tired and vulnerable and would be in no mood to deny the facts.

Overall, I was not in the mood to be bothered, and definitely had no energy to even question why I hadn't heard from Lamar. It was Tuesday, January 4th, 7 P.M., and I had spent the last couple of days, three days to be, exact tending to my family, being we had two deaths in the family back to back. A night I would never forget. During those moments I had witnessed Slim's consistency to be there when I needed him the most. Death was one hell of a way to start off the New Year but there were lessons to be taught during this distress I was experiencing. He had something to prove and nothing would stop him from leaving his mark.

I had just placed my phone on the charger and before I could even step one foot out of the room, Slim was calling. I hesitated before I answered. I answered the phone so rudely, he had to address me by my government name to make sure it was me.

He had concern in his voice.

He questioned why he hadn't heard from me.

He questioned whether or not I still wanted to fuck with him.

Acting as if he actually had a heart.

"*But why the fuck was he concerned about me?*"

He had a list of females he could tend to, so, "why was he calling me?" "*Why did it matter if we ever spoke again?*" "*Why did it matter why I hadn't call?*" I'm sure he knew exactly why, as most men, Slim thought he knew everything.

In the midst of the conversation this motherfucker had the nerve to blame me for some shit he involuntary gave me. He went from being a hoe ass nigga to apologizing for the mishap in seconds. And get this, he wanted to make it to up to me by taking me on a date.

THIS WAS NO ORDINARY DATE. This was not the normal dinner and a movie type date. This date was planned and well thought out.

Riddle me this. "*What hood nigga do you know that would actually take someone on a date with reservations already made?*" He scheduled to pick me up at 3 P.M. Wednesday evening, claiming he wanted to spend all day with me, and that's exactly what I gave him, all day. But to get me ready for it, he stopped by my house late Tuesday night to drop off some money so that I could pamper myself early Wednesday morning.

He paid for everything; my clothes, shoes, handbag, along with my hair, nails and make-up. He got me right, more put together than I had ever been and I was fucking ecstatic.

However, I refused to show my appreciation and negated to let him think that everything was all gravy. I was

Empress Hyder

bad-to-the-bone, my core was hard as stone and I refused to break at the charm of any man, especially Slim.

There I was making plans with another nigga, getting use to a feeling that felt familiar at the beginning of me and Lamar. Through the pain I was enduring and at a point in my life where I needed him the most, Lamar must've had his hands full, because I hadn't heard his voice at all. It may seem redundant by now and you may begin to question why I keep informing you that I hadn't talk to Lamar and how long it had been since the last time we spoke. Hell maybe you can make some sense of what the hell was so important that his relationship was barely on his mind and then let me know.

You would think he would be the first person to be by my side and help me through this but I would only be fooling myself to expect anything from him at this point. He sent me his condolences but ask me how much of his time I actually received outside of the spare of the moment text messages. I was becoming numb to the thought of even being with Lamar. It began to not even bother me that he hadn't called. Cause' maybe all that shit I said before were just thoughts.

It didn't register to me at all. "What type of "MAN", using the term lightly would want to go without seeing his girl?" Yet alone go without talking to her. "What type of "MAN" would just let your text messages, voice-mails and missed calls pile up like his schedule was too hectic to spare you a minute?"

Lamar made shit complicated but he was the typical nigga. He was stubborn, too damn prideful and refused to let a woman help him with anything. But why be in a relationship if you're going to try to get through everything alone. With everything in me I did not want to go back to this. My pride would let me keep dealing with any of this.

Everyone around me, swore we were doing well, they swore we had the perfect relationship but outside the social networks the picture was a bit blurred. We were barely making it and it was time to get right or get left.

I even considered not going out with Slim but why the fuck would I miss out on being treated. Lamar was where I wanted to be, sometimes, but Slim was what I needed to just kickback and be free.

I couldn't blame Slim for the damage done to my heart by Lamar, so I was taking a risk and took him upon his offer. You gotta know, with risk, you either succeed or fail. Needless to say consequences for my decisions were the least of my worries.

He was putting in time for another man's crime and I was being led to separate the new from the old. I was seeking better days. It was our day and I wanted it to be perfect. I reiterated those thoughts to myself over and over again until it came down to it.

My mom had just zipped up the back of my Halston Heritage Pleated-jersey gown. The red tent on this dress complimented my skin and my man for the day. Obviously he wanted the same because he arrived just on time.

If there was one thing I loved other than the scent of a man, honey, it was a punctual man. The salon he sent me to had everything going at once, so me being ready on time was a relief. I wanted to be a little different from any other

Empress Hyder

women he had come in contact with since we officially met. Again, I didn't want him to wait, hell that was just too old fashioned and played out, and I was anxious to see what was in store for the day anyway.

Ethan liked girls with curls. I referred to him as Ethan because this was the character he would be disguised as on this lovely evening. So that's exactly what I gave him, big, bouncy curls with highlights that accented my nail polish.

I kept it simple, and because I had a long nail-bed with some pretty healthy nails I went with a French manicure to keep it classy. My makeup was natural, with a nude lip. I hated make-up but I allowed the MUA to apply some gold eyeshadow to bring out my almond shaped eyes. My heels, however were the best part of my ensemble. They were a simple silhouette, classic shape, making them truly distinctive. These heels were my irresistibly strappy evening heels featuring an ankle strap enclosure with toe strap and 6.5" stiletto heel.

Now, everyone that knows me, knows I'm against an open toe heel, but I looked too damn good, and I was feeling too damn pretty to hold back now. You should've been there to witness the boost of confidence I gave myself, once I stepped into the mirror to make sure I looked just as good as I felt.

My mother gave me her approval, even though she may have just sent my life to hell, so with everything in me I strutted down the stairs so fierce, I don't even think he was ready for the monster he was creating.

Before I could get to the door the door bell rung. I knew Slim was outside but I wasn't informed that he was getting out to actually meet me at the door. I must admit this in fact did catch me off guard only because out of all the things I were used to, I can't say this was one of them.

"Cam, your date is at the door," my mom said as she approached the stairs heading towards her bedroom.

"I got it ma," I replied taking one last look in the mirror.

To my surprise my mom didn't even bother to come speak. Weird, because she usually wanted to meet everyone that came to her house whether it be for five minutes or five hours.

Knowing her, I'm pretty sure she was standing in my room, looking out of my opened window, watching his every move as he politely lifted me into this Black on Black 2011 Range Rover, like a gentleman. He even went as far to make sure I was buckled in before he locked the door and secured me in. All I could think to myself was, "where in the world, did all of this come from." Secondly, "how many females had he wined and dined?" Thirdly, Slim cleaned up real well, and smelt great. I was secretly losing my composure and my mind.

Dressed in a nice Express sateen lapel blazer, with a red fitted oxford shirt underneath he looked very classy and not overdone. The right dress pants were key, especially to me, because I loved a man with an athletic butt. He had on a pair of clean & classic stretch cotton photographer dress pants that draped and added enough comfort for his balls to breathe. They were a dark rinse, something that could be dressed up or down to be on the safe side if plans changed.

Empress Hyder

His wingtip oxfords gave me life. This man had a since of style. "But where did it come from?"

HE HAD VERSATILITY. He had everything and more, and I wanted to be his everything and more, because, I just wasn't use to this shit and it was only the damn beginning. The smell of his cologne took over the atmosphere in the car, putting me in a daze, just being in his presence had me high on life.

We hadn't even made it to I-45 yet, and he was in no rush to get us to our destination, but he was in charge. At least he thought he was, so I let this be his day to have his way like never before.

He had the volume of the radio set to 5, while "I should be" by Dru Hill played in the background, as if this song was the soundtrack to our Love Jones. Before entering the ramp, he leaned over and gave me a kiss on my cheek. He ran his fingers through my hair, and then complimented me on how good I looked. I thanked him with grace, and the look on his face gave off the impression that I was in for more than I could bargain for.

"I'll be obliged if you step outside
Because my ride is awaiting out date and
Of steak and a night cap
We mating awaking
By smells of perfume that I inhale
And then tell how well we raise hell on the dizzell
Satin sheets
Heat from your feet keep me warm
The mood is perfected by sounds from the storm..."

The melody of "Space Age Pimpin" by 8ball and MJG took over as we rode in silence. See, this silence I could handle, it wasn't awkward it was just understood we would save something to talk about over dinner. The next few hours spent with him would be why I would still find myself around in the future.

WE ARRIVED OUTSIDE OF ABACUS, one of the top restaurants in Dallas, Texas specializing in exquisite culinary creations and exceptional food service for more than ten years.

As a young woman who was not new to fine dining, thanks to my mom, I was well-rounded when it came to food, so I knew all about the best restaurants with great food. Abacus was located on McKinney Avenue, which as right in the heart of downtown and exactly 15 minutes from my house, so we weren't quite in each other's presence for too long.

This area was far too familiar for my liking but our evening had just begun. There were surprises being thrown around everywhere, starting as soon as we pulled into the car port to valet.

After being welcomed to Abacus, valet opened both the driver door and the passenger door, but in a stern voice Slim demanded me to not get out. So he got out first, walked around the Range Rover to my side and insisted on helping me out.

At this point, and being this was about the second time he acted as if I needed him, I became uneasy. I understood that he was a man and all. I understood he was trying to be the MAN and all, but I refused to become dependent of any nigga who felt that would be access to owning me.

    I owned my damn self, and he needed to get that shit under control quick. I was and still am the type that will bark back. He made it so easy to ruin the mood, but I promised to keep my cool no matter what, because if it got too bad, I didn't mind cutting this shit short and catching a cab back to the crib.

    I wanted to think nothing but positive thoughts. *"Like damn didn't a bitch deserve some peace every now and then?"* After spending days thinking self-defeating thoughts, here I was again making up excuses for the situation at hand. Maybe this was new to the both of us, maybe he was just as nervous as I was, but when they addressed him with a "Good Evening, Mr. Watkins," that gave off an instant signal that I wasn't the only one trying to be his only one.

    Now that I look back at our situation, I really don't think I wanted to be his at all. Maybe it had something to do with the direct fact that I knew he could take care of all of my wants knowing Lamar had all of my needs covered. At least most of the time he did.

    Anyway, the host lead us to what seemed to be a sectioned off room for private parties, but no one else was there but us. This was a state-of-the-art private dining room, adding a touch of romance, professionalism and enjoyment to our evening. Equipped with wireless internet, a plasma screen, and access to other AV needs, allowing Mr. Watkins and I to enjoy a delicious dinner and five-star service.

Not only was I honored, just a tad, but I was impressed. Not only did he clean up well but the man had exquisite taste. Then again he was eight years older than I was at the time, had been around the blocks a few times, so I'm sure he knew all the tricks of playing the cards right.

Our dinner lasted about an hour and a half. The conversation was heated and at an all-time high. Focusing on topics such as, the past, the present, and the future. We talked about life itself and the different back roads we've taken. He told me all about his childhood, his past relationships, and his children. He was interested as to why, unlike most women my age, I hadn't given birth to any of my own. That conversation ended in him telling me, how bad he wanted me, how much of the world he could give me, and how he wanted nothing in return from me but my loyalty, and so on.

"You look nice." He stated shifting the gears of our conversation.

"Thanks." I responded briefly before taking a sip of Brunello Di Montalcino, 2009. The wine alone ran $165.00 a bottle.

He forced me to dig deep into the pits of my soul and offer up information I had buried deep within myself for years. He even began to ask me about Lamar and how I was pretending to be in love, yet I was there with him.

"So what are your plans?" Slim asked.

"My plans for?" I retorted unsure of how he expected me to respond.

"It's clear you have a nigga, so are you happy?" He replied without any hesitation.

Empress Hyder

I wanted to tell him of course I was not happy and that was the only reason I was there with him but my facial expression said it for me.

"He makes me happy, don't get me wrong, but we have our flaws just like everybody else." I replied while avoiding to make any eye contact whatsoever.

Throughout the night, I kept wondering, was he really trying to get to know me, or was this his way to gather all the ammunition he needed to use against me when things got bad.

I couldn't knock the fact that the chemistry was definitely there. We were so caught up in the moment that we didn't even order food, we just recommended to have the chef send us his signature dinner plates.

Slim had an 8 ounce Comanche Buffalo tenderloin Filet served with McPherson sangioves butter and a side of wood grilled asparagus. I, on the other hand ordered their hickory grilled Scottish salmon served with acorn squash puree and baby turnips.

Our dinner was coming to an end and it was time for me to head back home because I had a lot of packing to get done before I returned to Prairie View.

After dinner, he thanked me for going out of my way and coming with him, as if I had a choice. Slim had other plans for our night and invited me to a hole-in-the-wall in South Dallas for some unexpected hood fun. It was his brother's 22nd birthday and he didn't want to ride alone so since I was with him, I was his lady for the night.

Man, this wasn't the usual fun I would get myself into, this was no Beamer's Night Club. This spot sat on the corner of Lamar and looked like every prostitute, drug dealer and killer had ran through this joint. I instantly began to second guess my decision but after sitting outside for about 30 minutes we decided to go ahead and show our faces. We sat in each other presence silently at first then he struck an interesting conversation in the midst of handing me a cup of Amsterdam mixed with cranberry.

    I could tell he thought he knew me very well, because he had my cranberry and vodka on deck, but I think he was just trying to get me loose to see what the night would bring. Slim was that type of nigga. He always had his best interest and only his at heart.

    He began buttering me up so that I would feel comfortable in this infested ass neighborhood. But who was I fooling I was from the Grove, however the south just wasn't my hood of choice.

    I wish I could go into detail about the many different topics we discussed in the car but that would take up a few pages and a lot of your time so to keep it brief and to the point the one that lead to me staying with him that night was of course none other than sex.

SLIM WAS SLICK WITH HIS WORDS, and his actions. We sat side by side with one of his hands on my knee. That one hand that kept caressing my thighs. That one hand that was tempted to touch my jewels but kept being stopped.

    The both of us were buzzing. As bad as I wanted to be touched the car just didn't permit enough space for anything to happen.

Empress Hyder

I kept talking to take my mind off of what I wanted to do to this man and what I wanted him to do to me. I was about to get myself into some deep shit, and I didn't have a care in the world at the moment.

Under his breathe multiple of times he would utter how sweet of a woman I would be if I gave him some mad knowledge. We would both burst out in laughter not knowing what our next move would be. But me, being the gambler I am, had to get mine first, so I utilized my reverse psychology skills that I learned in my introduction to psychology course back in fall 2009.

"How would you feel if I asked you to give me head in the front seat of this Range Rover?" I blurted out mid-conversation. The look on his face was priceless. He went from looking out the window to staring me in my face asking me what I would do if he pulled off my heel and raised my dress up.

"I'm up for the challenge, I'm a real nigga and we like to push our faces in it." He replied.

That was the type of shit I loved to hear. My blood pressure was rising because I knew any minute now I would feel the warmth and wetness I felt the first time him and I came face to face.

I readjusted my chair, turned my body towards him and slowly handed him my leg to see if he was about what he was talking about. He pulled my heel off with ease, lifted my dress up to my hips, pushed my legs apart and dived in. I swear I began to hyperventilate being that I already had it on my mind that something off the wall was going to happen in the back parking lot of this random ass hole-in-the-wall.

He performed so perfectly, as if he had it planned that he would make my last couple of nights in Dallas unforgettable. I mean I've had sex in a car before but not to this extreme and it was definitely spontaneous and shit like that drove me wild.

Once again my body became limp, as my juices began to run onto his leather seats. He turned on defrost so that the windows wouldn't fog. We wanted to avoid being as obvious as a Range Rover parked in the back of a building in South Dallas. But, he wasn't done yet. We weren't done yet. Because I had to get him back.

Sex, with us at this point had become a competition. While eating my pussy I just knew his dick was rock hard in those dress pants he had on. It worked out in our favor, because this was the right time to jump out of our formal attire and switch into something more comfortably and suitable for this late night detour.

The clock struck 12:15 A.M. and here we were making love to each other with our mouths like the world was about to end. I didn't want it to end.

His soul was interlocking with the nectar from my body and I was in heaven. The fact that I was getting head in the front seat of a Range Rover didn't make me nervous at all. This definitely was something I enjoyed and I was willing to hold my knees to my chest until he decided to come up for a fresh breath of air. I begin to rotate my hips in the opposite direction of his tongue. I wanted him to taste

Empress Hyder

everything I had. I wanted his face so far in it my juices would run down his chin.

I began to stroke his warm manhood with my left hand. By this time he had come up, licked his lips, and exhaled as if his taste buds had just been satisfied.

I could tell he felt like the man of the year, the one who didn't mind putting his face in it and I didn't mind giving his head a push. He took pride in a job well done.

The clock was ticking as he waited patiently in the driver's seat for his turn. By this time Kanye West 808s & Heartbreak was playing. I pulled my dress down, put my heels back on, gathered my thoughts and leaned over the arm rest. I sternly gripped his shit with my right hand, letting him know by my actions that tonight it belonged to me. Before I placed my mouth directly over the top of his dick, I took a deep breathe so that I would show no mercy.

I wanted this feeling to mimic the movement of full penetration. I wanted to stimulate his penis using my tongue, lips, and my mouth. I had to blow like a pro, like never before so I took his penis repeatedly into my mouth, with plenty of spit. Because I love that sloppy shit, I sucked up and down his shaft circling my tongue in a crazy 8 motion.

I was careful not to graze his 'friend' with my teeth. However though, I'm more than certain he had never had it like this before, and his moans were a sign I was the best yet to come.

I made love to him with my mouth. I showed him how pretty girls got down. I mean we were cracking down on time and I had to wrap this shit up, but I was enjoying it more than he was, hell sucking his dick was turning me on.

    Like never before, I was in my zone, and he was to. He gently pushed the top of my head down causing me to gauge, but I was far from an amateur, and deep throating was my specialty. I varied my rhythm, speed and intensity while I gently caressed his balls and then upped the pace for a few strokes.

    I was trying to take him to the edge then bring him back from the brink to get him revved up and eager for more.

I was in the groove and for about the last three minutes I licked, sucked and played with his erected penis using my tongue trying to bring him to his breaking point. I wanted him to cum in my mouth. Hell there was nowhere else for it to go. I wanted to try something new and he would be the perfect person to try it with.

    He had a crooked smile on his face as we made eye contact. To make sure I was hitting the spot, I watched his reactions closely. I tried to talk to him to see if he was enjoying it, but he was so into it he didn't say much.

    He was no Lamar, so I had to make sure I performed far beyond his standards. I'm sure he was thrilled that I wanted to know exactly how to please him. So to wrap our session up, I blew on it and kissed it one last time, signaling I was done.

    Slim's dick was so hard he could break down a brick and by the time he got his pants zipped and belt buckled, I had once foot out the car and his nosey ass brother was calling his phone trying to figure out where we were. Shit,

Empress Hyder

we were coming. Factually. At this point Slim was really beginning to move Lamar out of the picture.

He was trying to be the one who would give me what I deserved because deep down inside he knew the situation at hand. Slim was trying to be my man and he didn't give a damn about no one else and to what extent he went to prove his point. His goal was to push Lamar out the way by any means necessary and I no longer desired to put up a fight.

He leaned over and planted a romantic kiss right above my left eye before we got out the car and met at the front of the Range in the center of the headlights. He startled me when he placed his hands on my waist, but I had to remember he had to be in charge in all that he did, even something as simple as guiding me to the entrance of the club.

From the looks of the place on the outside I could tell I wouldn't fit in no matter how hard I tried. So I instantly attempted to come intact with my inner ratchet. You know, the hood chick I use to be before I got some class. I had to adapt before we stepped foot inside this joint and lean on not my own understanding as to why I had even agreed to join him in this after-hour festivity.

The place was BYOB which was not too far beyond my liking. The cover charge was five dollars a person, in which Slim paid for since I was his guest.

Ironically, my whole demeanor changed once we got inside this small little building they called "Side Lines". As soon as I hit the entrance it was as if everyone in the room stopped and gave me their undivided attention. The music began to play in slow motion and all eyes were on us. I felt a tap on my shoulder, coming from the waitress that offered me a free shot compliments of the owner.

I wanted to refuse it so bad but I figured that would have been rude. I glanced to the back of the building and spotted a cousin I hadn't seen in a minute so that relaxed my nerves just a little and I began taking shots to the head like no tomorrow. I didn't want to remember any of this in the morning, hell I didn't want to remember any of this by the end of the night.

No matter what, I had it in my mind that I would stay towards the front in case something popped off. There was so much shit going on in this place. You had certified hood niggas shooting dice and shooting pool at the same pool table to my left. You had the stripper, who looked like she needed to retire because no one was paying attention to her to at all. You had the bitches in front of me twerking and getting ready for the cage fight they were about to partake in. And here I was just sitting and waiting for Slim to return to me after wondering off to make his rounds.

From a distance he caught my eye and winked. Those shots of whatever had my body feeling tingly, him winking had my mind speculating and the DJ started to play my all-time favorite dance songs. So I had to show them how I got down.

"Spread ya Legs" one of the hottest songs in the clubs, by T Cash was playing throughout this spot and I instantaneously turned into the stripper buried deep within my dignity.

"Spread ya legs, let me see ya

Empress Hyder

Arch ya back, let me see ya
Bend ya knew, let me see ya
Spread ya legs, aye aye"

I was bending my knees and arching my back as the song implied and I could see the whole club watching. I was hitting every beat and drop, but niggas knew not to get too close.

"*Arch ya back, spread ya legs*
Got that aqua fina, she gone wet my bed"

The bitches were dry hating. I was stripper kicking and twerking in circles around them hoes. They stood no chances against me. "Ride My Face," was next up and I began to one leg twerk before dropping down to the floor and rotating my hips in a circle.

I was putting on the show.
I was calling everyone out.
I was letting Slim know he was about to get the business. He definitely was my target for the night as I sold every other man inside that joint a fantasy.

After dancing to the beat of my own drums, in my own world, keeping all eyes on me, I was becoming restless. Not restless as in sleepy but restless as in I was ready to move around.

Slim eased up behind me, so quietly, pressing his dick against my back sending nothing but impure thoughts racing through my thick ass skull.

He whispered in my ear, "I'm going to do damage when we get home."

"Where was this home he was talking about, because I had not agreed to go home with anyone?"

But you know just like I do, Slim knew he had me right where he wanted me, and No, Stop and don't do that were not in my vocabulary when it came to him. Anyway, as usual, I chuckled and pushed him away into the smoke that was consuming the room. I kept myself busy by engaging in a conversation with my cousin and touching on the ass of a stripper until it was time to go.

I became amazed how someone so much older in age could still work the pole with so much poise and dignity. She stood with confidence in her 8 inch platform heels, working hard for nothing more than one dollar bills. We made eye contact across the room, guessing that signaled her to come to where I was standing. She tried to teach me new tricks as if I needed any, but I was all for learning new skills and techniques to add to my package. All I could think about was how she got here. "What possessed her to want to stoop this low as if this was some type of career?" I mean I had always thought about tapping into stripping for solely the income, nothing more nothing less, but my pride wouldn't let money rule everything around me. I stood for more than that shit and was not about to fall victim to anything but cocaine before I could even catch myself.

From a distance it looked as if Slim was enjoying himself. He would randomly come over to check on me and to make sure nobody was getting out of line, but I was fitting in just fine, for once in my life. From left to right I was being handed shit mixed with everything and anything. I was feeling too good and he knew we were about to get it in all night long. Luckily, no one was paying us any mind because we were cutting up and didn't give a damn who saw. I

Empress Hyder

fucked with him and he fucked with me and what was understood wouldn't need to be explained to anyone outside of us.

The night was cracking down, the clock stuck 2:45 A.M. and it was time to move around. We said our goodbyes to those who came and left and witnessed the looks on everyone's face who watched us walk out the club hand in hand. That moment, in the midst of our exit, was everything.

We finally made it back to our car and drifted away in the darkness of the South Dallas back roads. His right turn at the stop sign of South Lamar let me know that he had no intentions of taking me directly home.

I was down for whatever, as long as it would give me peace and quiet. I was tired of the outsiders and I wanted some us time because we all know what came along with that. Plus, we had to finish what we started; especially since my panties were already soaked from just pondering on what would go down once he got me to a bed.

Out of all street in Dallas, *"why did we have to be making moves on pavements that reminded me of him?"* Him being Lamar, and these pavements were ones I had siked myself to believe I was no longer willing to chase.

The fact that I would be leaving soon constantly reminded me why his presence was appreciated. I entered into an experience of weakness and powerlessness, became part of the uncertainty, and gave up my self-control and self-determination.

Thoughts of Lamar began to surface to my mind being in three days I would be back to the life I left behind when I headed home for a much needed break.

The girl in me wanted to ask Slim to take me home, because I knew the end wouldn't end so well. However, the woman in me wanted Slim to give me all that he had to offer. From that day forward, I wanted to be the Bonnie to his Clyde. I didn't want to be without him. I didn't want to live without him. I didn't want to go without him. In reality I think I just didn't want to be alone.

But what was a girl supposed to do when someone so charming was sweeping you off your feet in the midst of the biggest down fall ever to occur in life thus far.

My world wasn't even upside down, I was well aware of what was going on, but I wasn't ready to end neither situation with either of them. My mind was carrying heavy burdens of my past, and I was bound to experience more of the same. They say the past perpetuates itself through lack of presence. However, the quality of my consciousness at this moment is what was shaping my future.

That car ride had me as timid as a fawn taking its first steps into adulthood away from the comforting warmth of its mother's side. I was literally shitting bricks because even if I wanted to reconsider he already had his devil horns inside the rib cage akin to the one I formed from.

The traffic on TX-183 forced me to tap into my inner poet and write out my thoughts so that I wouldn't be mentally lost on this road I was traveling. The words just began to flow as if the poem was already written. As if this story had already been told. As if it already had an ending.

Empress Hyder

My thoughts played out a little something like this as I decided to type my feelings into a notepad app I had downloaded onto my phone.

> I am overflowing with emotion
> my cup runneth over
> over love, or so I thought I was
> I once thought I was over Lamar
> but, even I can fool myself; shame on me
> a fool of me to believe
> what I knew in my heart wasn't true
> lies covered in makeup
> fables used to conceal the truth
> your lips, spread like the Red sea
> and fallacies come out
> I'm current out.....
> my mind
> In my mind,
> I'll always be his lady
> You got me going crazy
> or maybe just crazy in love
> cause I would have given
> the world to you
> the Sun, the moon, & the stars too
> but you were like the Sky to me
> you would shine light
> and brighten up my night life
> and I would have went to the edge of the Earth for you
> fell off,
> and then dust myself off
> and proceeded to try again
> I would try again and again
> over and over again
> trying until I got it right

I lost my right...
to love me fully
I surrendered my heart,
I surrendered my love over to a man that was still foreign to me
Against my will, it was like I had no choice
I had to
Voodoo.
You had me under your spell
Put a root on me
I guess, he has his hooks in me
Addicted.
You were like my first hit of that good shit
and I've been hooked since then
An addict.
You were that one drug momma warned me about
You.....are.....a beautiful nightmare

    Tears randomly began to fall, and as I tried to wipe the pain and shame away, he placed his right hand on my left thigh and said in a reassuring voice, "Everything is going to be ok".

    With no clue of what was going on, or where it would go from here, with any heads-up or a fair warning, we had finally arrived to our destination for the night, The Gaylord Texan Resort and Convention Center. *"This nigga here!"*

    This wasn't anything I wasn't use to outside of casual fun with my mom, but to have a man that knew how to wine and dine a woman that was a different story. Slim was beginning to grow on me for all the right reasons that

Empress Hyder

seemed so wrong. I mean, I deserved to get this treatment. I deserved to be the center of somebody's world. But I didn't want to be in so deep, I began to lose myself in the mist of lust and temporary happiness, knowing we too could end up like Lamar and I. Everything about him was different, but I was not to be fooled. Some men were known to take the mind and keep the body. A form of mental slavery, if you know what I mean. But I wasn't in the mood to be a philosopher, I just wanted to enjoy that night and worry about tomorrow when it came.

We valet the car and walked hand-in-hand to the entrance of the hotel lobby.

"Nice to see you Mr. Allen." The valet said aloud as he accepted the keys from Slim.

"Alright now boss, watch my whip." Slim replied.

Their exchange of conversation for the split second made me realize Slim was a regular. *"Who was he bringing here or who had he brought here before me?"*

"You two enjoy your night," another valet stated as he opened the passenger door and assisted me out.

When we entered the lobby the excitement that overcame my body was that of a toddler in a candy store. My eyes were naturally drawn upward to the magnificent frescoed ceiling. There, in all its glory, was a collaboration forged by some of Europe's' most celebrated painters, sculptors and craftspeople. The nerd in me wanted to tap into my inner genius and tour the lobby and all its amazing artwork but I had my own craft to master in the penthouse.

Did you catch that, he got us the penthouse suite. He was molding me into a Queen, his Queen of the damned.

The elevator ride up felt like the car ride to get here. I was tired of being mobile and was ready for some action that required me lying down.

He pressured me to being the first to enter the suite. I knew at the point, yet again he had something up his sleeve. The night had been full of surprises and had me sort of curious as to what it was all about.

This was the most luxurious accommodations and one of the most impressive suites I had ever seen. I think he out did himself with that one. At 3,500 odd square feet, this suite featured a king size bed in the bedroom, a separate living room with fireplace and grand piano, a den, and up to three connecting rooms to make it a four-bedroom suite. The suite also featured a sound system which just so happen to be playing one of my favorite old school jams, "You" by Jesse Powell. Chills begin to form all over my body because I couldn't figure out what was going through his head as he stood against the wall just soaking in this moment. He didn't make any sudden movements, he just looked at me with that look, and you know that look someone gives you when they know they've proved their point, yes that look. I digressed in every form possible because he was definitely winning. And I was losing.

Losing me more than anything, but it would be nothing for me to recollect if this just so happened to be more than I could bare.

My first mind directed me to the bed. But my gut directed me to the bathroom. A bathroom with a bathtub surrounded with lavender candles and filled with the most delicate rose petals a girl could ever lay her eyes on. At that point I was on the verge of having a fucking anxiety attack.

He was giving me so much, so soon and I could not pinpoint why. *"What was it about me that was making Slim become who he was becoming?"* This shit, falling in loving or even thinking you wanted to be with someone to this extent took months not hours. So I just sat there. Confused. Attempting to try to figure things out.

I could barely even see the water. I was so distracted by how beautiful the red reflection of the roses glistened in the mirror I didn't even realize Slim had walked up behind me. He startled me when I felt a kiss on my neck and the next one on my cheek. I was so dazed that Slim asking me to marry him hadn't even clicked just yet.

Chapter Seven

Empress Hyder

"Everything had come into sharp focus: his smooth words, his black, glinting eyes, his broad experience with lies, seduction, and women. I'd fallen in love with the devil."

— Becca Fitzpatrick

◈ ◈ ◈

I turned around slowly so that I could take in what was happening. Only to find slim on one knee behind me with the biggest rock I had ever laid my eyes on. He had tears in his eyes as if he wanted me to say nothing other than yes. The fear passing through my thrust felt like I was swallowing stones causing me to forcefully say aloud, *"Let me think about it...I just need to think about it."* The aura of the room changed.

"What the fuck do you mean think about?" I could tell he was angry by the tone of his voice.

"It's either a yes or a no." He stated repeatedly.

"There's nothing to think about." He growled.

With the look of disappointment on his face he sat the custom engagement box on the vanity above the tub. He pushed himself passed me and slammed the door behind him.

As a woman who had an idea of how she wanted everything to go when the time came, this proposal wasn't ideal.

Leaving me no choice to do exactly what I didn't want to do. Think. As a woman, I yearned to be loved and treated as if I was the only one. But in reality that was never and would never be the case.

Just like marriage, for me, probably would never be the case for me. I mean marriage was something I felt I was supposed to desire. Just like giving birth to a child and

Empress Hyder

nurturing the environment. As a woman, everything about life was to be given. Being born a woman transitioning into a wife was a blessing to come, because as the bible said, Proverb 18:22, *"He who finds a wife finds a good thing and obtains favor from the LORD."*

Companionship was to die for literally, hence the vow "until death do us part". *"But was I really ready?" "Was I ready to take that vow after only a month of going steady with Slim?"* Not to mention we were still not alone. I wasn't even sure if Lamar and I were really done yet. Every chance I got, I found myself sending text messages letting him know I loved him more than I did yesterday, truly meaning every word. Something had a hold on me.

"Was it even possible to love two men at the same time?" I understood Lamar and I no longer stayed together and we were going different places in life but in the midst of the storm there had to balance. For once we needed to have a plan for our relationship or the relationship I wanted us to have. We rarely talked and In his absence Slim was filling the void. I really didn't know what the foundation of our relationship consisted of. At the end of the day, he had a girl when we met and I was on the verge of being dumped by my ex. I knew he was dealing with his own personal problems but so was I and I still managed to make the essential time for him. There were times I had to call Lamar five times and allow nine hours to pass by before he would even return my call. I sat around assuming shit when I could have been out doing God knows what.

Lamar wasn't making it hard for me not to fuck around. Good morning text messages had ceased and when

I checked my phone before the sun was to rise it would be the continuation of whatever the fuck we were talking about the night before. I didn't even want to go back to school to get my shit from his room, only to move into my apartment in Houston because I couldn't bear seeing his face.

    I admit it came days where shit between Lamar and I would get heated and I just knew it was the end. The disrespect was at an all-time high. I was being ignored and deep down inside I really believe I had had enough. I shed not one tear because everything had begun to bottle up for so long. I grew tired of repeating the problems I was having, why I was so unhappy knowing this nigga couldn't even tell me what we needed to do to fix it.

    I agree I said some things I didn't mean but in the heat of the moment I wanted him to hurt just like I did. Although we were apart I always tried my best physically and mentally to be there for him but he never seen that shit. All he focused on were my assumptions, constant nagging and flaws. He never heard the cry for help. Lamar never got the point that all I wanted was his attention and for him to prove to me he wanted to be there. Trust me, I didn't mean bombard me with a million text messages, but at least show interest in how my day was going or how I slept. The shit your nigga is supposed to do. And all the shit I expected from him, Slim was doing without having to be told.

    It all ended over the three words, no one wants to hear in a relationship, "I don't know". I asked him, were we going to make it five years or were we going to call it quits and this nigga had the nerve to tell me, he didn't know. As a woman, I did not and could not take that shit lightly,

Empress Hyder

because mentally, physically and emotionally I had given this man my all. I was exhausted. True enough, I was hard on him, but what woman wouldn't be if you could see the potential that your man had within, yet he was just having a hard time utilizing it. That shit became stressful. There were many nights I sat up and cried because I felt like for all these years, I was settling. We had nothing in common. His life consisted of going to rodeos, tending to his animals and football. My life consisted of studying, writing, and shopping. He and I were nothing alike. I knew I was losing him because it was all in his actions whereas, he would always blame me for pushing him away. In the long run, what are you to do when your back is against a wall, your man is three hours away, the calls have stopped, the text messages are no longer getting responded to, and your effort isn't being matched. You lash the fuck out, which was exactly what I did. I had no problem telling him how I felt, because I deserved the same treatment. I deserved to be with someone who knew my worth just as well as I did. Someone who didn't mind fulfilling his duties as "the man" in our relationship. I didn't have time for no fucking man boy, and as much as I loved him, I just wanted him to grow the fuck up and be the man I needed him to be. Reality was Lamar would only be the man he was, and obviously he wasn't the one for me. I'm not impressed by pizza-hut dates but I went with the flow being at the time that's all he could afford. Maybe I was out of his league, but after 4years you would think he would have adapted to my qualifications by then.

I knew one day we would grow apart. However, Slim couldn't have been the blame for it all, because the fight and the arguments always got the best of our relationship when we were hundreds of mile away from one another.

I do not understand and still fail to comprehend how anyone survives a long distance relationship. Distance did not make our hearts grow fonder. Not one bit. The anxiety I went through not knowing where he was, who he was with, and what he was doing, mentally drove me insane.

I didn't trust him as far as I could see him, especially when I was well aware of his capabilities. Flashbacks of all the bad times Lamar and I experienced, had me scared stiff trying to make a decision.

"What did I really know about Slim?"

"Was it enough to make a decision I would grow to regret?"

"Was I really and wholeheartedly the chosen one out of everyone trying to be the one?"

I stood with my feet firmly planted on the foreign designer rug that was laying perfectly on the marble bathroom floor hoping he would leave me where I was. Trusting he would not disturb this moment I was using to reflect on what use to be. That moment was everything I needed to revisit on the memories I never wanted to forget.

Everything I wished for as a little girl was surfacing but the woman in me, well the woman I was becoming was screaming, "DON'T DO It," from the pits of my sacred soul. Nonetheless, knowing Slim admired my vulnerability and confidence in him, I gathered myself together with an ocean of tears rolling down my face. Before reaching for the door I grabbed the satin white gown that sat folded neatly next to the sink.

I took multiple deep breaths and wiped the tears from the wells of my eyes. I would have to face him either way, so it was then or never.

"Yes!" I said as I approached the corner of the bed.

"What?" He replied, uninterested in what I had to say.

"Yes, I will marry you Ethan." I responded as I reached for his hands. He pulled me in for a hug and we just stood there.

I had never witnessed a perfect marriage even though my great-grandparents would have been married almost 50 years. Bless their hearts. A godly relationship, wrapped in the affairs my great-grandfather had with his mistresses. Even with all the illegitimate children that entered their lives my grandmother stood by my grandfather's side as any good Christian wife would. She knew the man she married so she handled each situation with grace. Despite the betrayal and the broken vows, she chose to keep her marriage sweet. With his sins lying deep inside the walls other women. Those women he would never love nor acknowledge in public. Though my grandfather was deacon, his heart was pure yet his pants were dirty. No doubt in my mind he didn't love his wife but temptation came from the devil himself. As a man of God he was a target, as most men are. However free will should remind you that you have a wife at home.

I had my concerns. So, I, even with this ring on my finger, would always be aware that Slim was a man first. A man who could have any woman he wanted, because unlike myself some bitches just wanted to be kept. That mentality was one I would never understand. It is a man's world but damn, did it have to consist of more than one bitch in it.

Reflecting on my past with Lamar, I don't think I'd ever been the only one and that shit was something that had to change. Especially when you go to war and bat for a nigga who let every female run around speaking on his name. Seriously, "when do the games stop and when are the fucks given?" You try your best to deal, because things like this happen, but it was really starting to bother me. Knowing I've given my all to someone in the past who threw it all away because of the mishaps in his life. Then again Slim had me. He had me just where he wanted me. From day one he was doing everything in his will to break me, train me and mold me into the person he wanted me to be. Deep down inside I knew he popped the question knowing that a growing women like myself would only be submissive to her husband. But one thing he hadn't learned nor seen yet was that I was quick to walk away from anyone without any explanation.

In that moment, I wanted what I wanted and it was most definitely him. No second guessing, no stressing and I didn't care what anyone had to say about it.

I became an emotional wreck. I just wanted to lay on his chest, wrapped in my gown granting enough time to take in this moment. I slowly began to drift into a daze. My eyes were fighting to stay open. Every muscle in my body started to relax as I inhaled the scent of his cologne. Until my phone started to go off. I began getting text messages. Someone had left me a voice mail. My inbox was overflowing with messages on Facebook, back to back like an emergency was taken place. *"What the fuck was really going on?"*

Within five seconds my question was answered when I opened a message from Renay, just mentioning her trifling ass has ruffled my feathers, but that's a story for another day.

Renay: "Girl, check your Facebook"

Me: "I'm busy, I'll hit you later." I replied with an automated response saved in my phone.

Renay: "Would you do it now, you really need to see this."

Me: Send me a picture.

Renay: Attachment: 4 Images

There it was, like a thief in the night, coming to still the little joy I had left. A picture of Lamar and I guess his new bitch having a movie night for the motherfucking world to see. It just didn't register to me, how three days before the end of a four year relationship, Lamar managed to find someone new. It was almost as if he had given up on our relationship a long time ago and was just letting it run is course until I got tired. He stopped putting forth the effort. His moods would change frequently. One day he goes without even picking up the phone. Then the next day he is calling me just to hear my voice.

For all they knew, Lamar and I were still together and like a coward, he decided to stunt on me over a social media network. The only female who saw him at his lowest points and he got down on me like that. I was livid and ready to make my way to Houston, despite the fact I was now officially engaged.

I tried to find my inner peace, since I had begun practicing meditation and shit. I tried to refrain from being quick to anger because I might have behaved in a way that was beyond unladylike. Ironically, my last conversation with Lamar via text message focused on him being free. He kept repeating how he just wanted to focus on getting his money right, mastering his craft in the aspect of football, and getting himself together. At this point in his life he just couldn't give me what I needed and I just needed to let go. He kept going on about why I wasn't for him and how it was not me it was him. That bullshit niggas say when they know they're foul. He even had the nerve to say he just didn't want a relationship right now and he thought we should just be friends. All of that said, just 3 days before he pulled this shit.

I could feel Slim staring at me out the corner of my eyes. Sensing something was bothering me, he instantly pulled me closer to him and began massaging my shoulders tracing the outline of my arm down to my hands that were placed gently on my thighs. He grabbed my left hand, and begin to suck my fingers one by one.

Everything paused for a split second at least that's what it felt like. Slim reached down and pulled a tray from the side of the bed.

"Umm, what is that?" I questioned curiously. I knew what it looked like but I didn't want to make any assumptions.

Empress Hyder

"What does it look like he?" He asked before snorting the first line of coke from the glass tray.

"Oh hell no Slim, I'm not about this life at all." I replied.

"Just try it, I promise it's not that bad." He insisted.

I wanted to tap into this moment but I couldn't get comfortable for the life of me. My body began to tense up and the tears started to form again. I was emotionally unstable.

I turned my head to gaze out of the window, admiring the city, just in case one a tear decided to fall. This was supposed to be my moment dammit. A night to remember. Unforgettable memories. My history in the making. Then again, *"who was I trying to fool?"* I took Slim up on his offer and snorted one of three lines of coke like a champ. My nose began to tingle. I could feel it in my throat. But I hit a second one and then a third.

Lamar was all I knew and to even think about him being in between the legs of another bitch made my flesh crawl. Lamar was all I had, and without him, the Camille Jones I am today would be irrelevant. It took every nerve in my body to calm the sense of anger that had taken over the ecstasy in the atmosphere. Meditating in the heat of this disturbing act, just wasn't cutting it for me. Slim's keys were sitting on the Ottoman at the edge of the bed and Houston was only three hours away but I could've made it in two hours without any stops.

Prepared to curse him out, his momma out and whoop her ass, I had to collect my thoughts to see if he was really worth it. Honestly, I don't think he was ever worth it. I reached for my phone and called just to see if he would answer. And like the bitch nigga he could be he let it go to voice-mail the first two times. Lord, Lamar knew I was ignorant and once I became furious nothing and no one could stop me.

I called a maximum of three times and he knew that was my limit. By the third time he managed to pick up the phone with a fucking attitude like he was the victim. I started spitting bullets from the time he said hello.

"So that's what we do?" I asked without giving him a chance to respond. Playing coy he acted as if he didn't know what I was referring to.

"Oh, that shit, man that's just Jasmine and she stopped by to see me while I was in town." Lamar knew damn well, that friendly shit was not going to fly with me, especially after all the lies he had told over the years. The funny thing about it though, he even tried to explain how long they had been talking, not realizing he was only telling on himself. Per my request he managed to screenshot a picture of their conversation. On this particular date in the photo, when he was supposed to be sleep, he managed to be texting another female, yet ignoring me. Maybe at that very instant, the thrill was really gone.

Lamar and I had been apart before, but we had never been here. We had never been to the point to where there seemed to be no solution to making it right, especially with my return being in two days. Nevertheless, it all began to make sense, for the both of us I'm sure, but as far as I knew, Slim was still a secret.

I had never really cheated to this extent before, a couple of dates, here and there, but that was it. My definition of cheating was never to the extent of being with another man. Hell, if I did give my time to another man; it was nothing a few white lies couldn't fix and knowing how jealous Lamar could be lying become a habit.

THE SITUATION AT HAND WAS DOWNRIGHT DISRESPECTFUL. Not to mention this chick was younger than him, already in love with him after maybe a week, and didn't and wouldn't compare to me at the end of the day. They even had cute little nicknames for each other. So from the outside looking in, this was a friendship brewing into a relationship. A relationship that would slowly but surely push me to go on about my business, following Lamar's lead. I assumed that's what he needed. Lamar thrived and lived for the attention of women, especially a woman that was not his own already.

The clock struck 3:30 A.M. and it was definitely time for me to call it a night snuggled upright next to my new fiancé. Without any hesitation, I forced my lips into the crease of his neck and begin to tug at his earlobe. No intentions of leading to sex, I just wanted to soothe my thoughts and to see if he was awake. I needed his undivided attention but he was paying me no mind. At this point in our relationship, I could tell when something was wrong, but having an attitude at this time of morning was something I was just not in the mood for.

Although, the frown on his face and the way that perfectly arched eyebrow was raised made my pussy extremely wet, I wanted rest more than anything.

He let out a deep sigh and pulled me closer, knowing that this phase would be one we would have to conquer together. Slim hopped out the bed and I could tell it bothered him, by the way he paced back and forth across the room. Though our situation was not unknown to him I'm sure he would've wanted me to deal with it some other time. If he could, he would have blocked Lamar's number a long time ago, but that was none of his doing to be done. Besides, from the moment I said yes, Slim and I had a whole future ahead of us and Lamar was definitely something that was to be left in the past.

Please understand, I laid down with Slim not knowing if I would ever get back up. Tossed all around the sheets with a soul-jerking fear that only a stone-cold killer could produce. We fucked like our lives depended on it, because in reality that was all we had. Calling it everything but lust, we thought we were in it for the long run. No desires to break-up or be apart we had nothing but our words and faith that we would make this thing last.

This would be our last night together and back to Prairie View I had to go. I was a totally different person. Change was in full effect at the moment I accepted this ring. I knew then I had to mentally prepare myself to balance this new addition to my life.

I was making a decision to take control of my life all while praying that this time around it would all be worth it.

Empress Hyder

    I do not even recall the topic of the conversation, Slim and I were having before he planted three kisses along my face. For someone who was abandoned he had a lot of love to give. He kissed me on my forehead, followed by the word I. The second one on my cheek, followed by the word Love and the last one on my lips followed by the word you. He was definitely affectionate that was for sure and before I could close my eyes to get at least 5 hours of sleep before it was time to check -out, Slim had yet another surprise for me.

    He reached under the pillow and grabbed a box that held two keys. I swear there was absolutely nothing I could put passed this man. Every chance he got he was dropping out for me. This was definitely something I yearned for but made a vow to myself that if the opportunity presented itself, make sure it was Godly in ways more than one.

    I thanked him, not knowing what the keys were for and honestly did not care because my body was giving out. Rest was the only thing on my mind while reaching across his body to turn off the lamp after he refused to do so. I drew a breath of strength, and then I was out cold. Until the 8:00 A.M. alarm sounded.

    In which my inner being questioned, *"who the fuck set an 8:00 alarm"*?

January 15th, 2011

Empress Hyder

"I can only note that the past is beautiful because one never realizes an emotion at the time. It expands later, and thus we don't have complete emotions about the present, only about the past."

— Virginia Woolf

◈ ◈ ◈

I stroke this keyboard all night and day to paint the imperfect picture of what my life has become these past two years.

Continually, taking you on a trip down memory lane, I can feel the twins going to war inside my brittle womb. As painful as the kicks and punches have been they have been a constant reminder of why I had to find the strength to pick myself up from that cold hardwood floor that night. The thought of losing my baby without knowing there were two was the reason I found the strength to fight back. I managed to flee the scene with nothing but the clothes on my back.
 Out of the four of us that were inside of that house, one of us didn't make it out. Who knew heading back down I-45 would be the turning point of the woman I was on a mission to become.

Hell, who knew heading back down what once was my road to freedom would be the same route running me straight to Slim's cell of isolation and abuse.

The sun was shining at an all-time high as I cruised down I-45. I had just passed the exit on the highway right before Madisonville, when the brake lights of the car ahead of mine flared. I slowed down, slowed some more, then had to press down on my breaks really hard to avoid running into the back of this old ass Honda with my newly washed Dodge Charger. As I crested the hill, traffic came to a complete stop, a long ribbon of taillights flashing red and white.

Empress Hyder

This was the perfect opportunity for me to call-up Renay, for two reasons, one to inform her I was heading back, and two to tell her I would be starving when I arrived. It took her all of 15 seconds to pick-up the phone as if she was busy or some shit.

"Hello", she yelled in the phone.

"Bitch, you better act like you miss me", I barked back.

"Anyway, I'm exiting Madisonville, I'll be on the Yard in about an hour or so," I added.

In which she replied without putting up a fight, "Ok girl, and stop by the store and get me some milk.

"*Bright lights, fancy restaurants*
Everything in this world that a man could want
Got a bank account bigger than the law should allow
Still I'm lonely now
Pretty faces from the covers of the magazines
From their covers to my covers wanna lay with me
Fame and fortune still can't find
Just a grown man runnin' out of time
Even though it seems I have everything
I don't wanna be a lonely fool
All of the women, all the expensive cars
All of the money don't amount to you
So I can make believe I have everything
But I can't pretend that I don't see
That without you girl my life is incomplete"

Singing to the top of my lungs, with my radio maxed out at the volume of 38; I hadn't even recognized Slim had called me three times. As I went to return his call, a sense of unsureness came across my heart, and I returned my focus to my iPhone to continue listening to Incomplete. In order to knock out this trip I indulged in a mini concert. This usually made the rime pass by much faster.

    Slim: "Call me when you can."

    Me: "Ok."

    Going about 80 miles down the back roads I was 10 minutes away from the freeway. I was anxious to get back to my other life but nervous to face my truth.

    As I pulled into the MSC parking lot, I looked nothing like the girl I was when I left. I parked my car taking up two lanes, because the last thing I needed was for someone to dent my shit.

    Everywhere was a stage and a runway for me, so as soon as I stepped one foot out the door, motherfuckers were all on my jock. I knew I was the shit and I carried myself accordingly, with my stacked bob, natural makeup, #82 eyelashes, and a fitted two-piece Nike outfit that my ass sit just right and my Nike flip-flops. Shit got real on the road, so you know a bitch had to be as comfortable as possible. Fuck trying to be cute and shit and just in case I ran into Lamar, I had to be able to move around swiftly.

    I briefly acknowledged the group of niggas that sat outside the sliding doors in front of the Memorial Student Center shooting dice. Slowly made my rounds into the game room, where all of the PV locals were talking loud and boastfully playing dominos. It felt good to be back on the Yard for the time being.

    Heading towards the restroom, out the corner of my eye, I could see Lamar posted up in front of the bookstore

Empress Hyder

with his teammates. With everything in me I could not let him see me sweat, but I know he knew my ass from a mile away so I kept walking. I hesitated for a minute, hoping he would call my name, but the way his attitude was set up he would not give in. He was too prideful and I was beyond stubborn, so the circle game was the one we would choose to play. I stood in front of the restroom mirror, my hands shaking with anxiety because I knew it would come to this, I was just hoping not so soon. I touched up my makeup and reapplied my Retro Matte Mac lipstick before the group of Panther Dolls piled into the restroom stalls.

I gathered my things from the counter and mentally prepared myself to come face to face with Lamar. It was like he timed my exit because as soon as I turned the corner, I heard a familiar voice behind me.

"So you weren't going to speak," Lamar asked.

"Speak for what?" I replied.

He continued to press the issue, as if I was the one who fucked this all up. I could feel waterworks forming in the shafts of my eyes, and in the same moment, my phone began to vibrate.

"Excuse me." I said stepping away, leaving him with this blank stare on his face. I had to concentrate on finding my phone in the bottom of my purse. It was Renay probably getting ready to ask me had I made it. At least I thought that's who it would be.

"Hello," I yelled in the phone.

"Come outside," Slim demanded.

Confused, I stared at the screen of my phone for a matter of five seconds. Reason number one being, *"why in the fuck was Slim calling me from Renay's phone?"* Reason number two, *"what the fuck was really going on?"*

The only two things I grew curious about were how the fuck did either of them know where I was and why in the fuck was he not in Dallas.

But no worries, it was time to get to bottom of this shit, so as cool, calm, and collective as I could remain, I headed outside only to find Slim parked directly behind my car talking to Renay in the parking lot. There was attitude in every step I took, and I knew they could see me coming. Somebody, hell, either he or she was about to let me know what was really up, whether they knew it or not. And nobody was departing until I got the answers I were looking for.

As of now I sure you can tell I am a territorial female. Not on purpose but just a hormonal control of ones aggression about what belonged to me. Far from jealous, because the nigga was already mine. My trust was just fucked up and I didn't trust Slim nor did I trust any bitch as far as I could see him or them.

Now, don't get me wrong, Renay was my girl and all, but we've had too many "unintentional" run-ins about my niggas. She had burnt me once, so only time would tell before she would try me again. And I wasn't just gone place my nigga dick in her hand willingly.

We hadn't gone through shit together just yet, and I'd be damn if he would get away so easily.

"What chu bout to do?" Slim asked aggressively.

"Head to the library, what's up?" I replied.

Empress Hyder

"I need you to ride to Houston with me; I'll have you back in an hour."

After being in the car all day, I was ready to eat, smoke and chill. Damn, *"could a bitch just rest for one second?"* I was not in the mood for being around his ass all day, especially after thinking he was in Dallas where I left him.

"Houston, for what?" I responded with a stiff neck.

"CJ, you coming or what?" He questioned.

"Since when did he start calling me CJ?" I mean, I kind of liked it, at least the way he said it, all hostile and everything but I still was against riding.

I swear I hated giving in to him but I couldn't resist him. I wanted him right that second and not one second later. I tried to figure out what could be so important to where it could not wait. Then again, he had me anxious to see how the ride to Houston would play out.

I put my phone on Do Not Disturb at least until we made it to where we would be in Houston. Switched out my lipstick and relaxed. Car rides with Slim were always interested so I looked forward to the unexpected. I wanted him to touch me. Hell I wanted to feel it and I didn't want my hotline to start jumping being I had just touched back down.

I remember letting the seat as far back as it could go and placing my hand around his neck so that I could play with his left ear. Every attempt to turn him on as much as possible. Within seconds he mashed the gas and I just knew we were going 100 miles per hour down highway 290.

Everything was good just like it was supposed to be. Although, it was kind of awkward riding in complete silence. That was a first, nonetheless I just took it as him plotting as usual. I found the urge to sit up, unzip his pants and plant the print of my brand new Bao Bao Wan, Lavender Jade MAC lipstick on his Lacoste boxers.

With each lick to his scrotum I could feel all the tension releasing from his body. If I wanted to keep this man, I had to please him anywhere and everywhere. I just knew he deserved it, or maybe this was all part of his well thought out plan. He had my mind gone and I could feel my sense of self shifting, but again everything was so good, *"why fuck it up now?"*

Forty minutes of straight sloppy toppy and nowhere to spit. My only option was to swallow every ounce of his nut and that's the only part I hate about performing the art of dick-sucking.

The scenery went from dim to lite, and we were coming to a stop. Gently pulling my head up and running my thumb across the bottom of my lip to remove any residue, I noticed we were pulling up to a gas station. Something about this gas station looked all too familiar. For whatever reason at this very moment, I could feel pressure on my bladder from being nervous. Butterflies uncontrollably rumbling through my system. I could feel the knots in my stomach and a lump forming in my throat. *"Why in the fuck were we here out of all places to be in Houston?"*

Chapter Eight

"Tension, in the long run, is a more dangerous force than any feud known to man."

— Criss Jami, *Killosophy*

Empress Hyder

◆ ◆ ◆

As I stepped foot out of the car, I heard a familiar voice yell out, *"Chameleon, girl is that you?"* I damn near froze where I was standing, scared to look over my shoulder to see if Slim was still around. I knew exactly who it was. The only person to call me Chameleon. Luckily Slim had already gone into the store, so I was definitely ok to acknowledge him.

All I could think to myself was holy shit. I knew damn well, the gentleman yelling out my name was not Larry. Larry the fucking crack head. The same fucking Larry who use to come to Lamar momma's house and clean up the kitchen so that he could take home the leftovers. This nigga would feed the fucking leftovers to his dog. A dog named Mister.

I could not be believe that was happening. I had to be day dreaming, because before I knew it Larry was heading in my direction looking confused. As far as he knew I belonged to Lamar and that's all he wanted to know.

I fumbled with the door handle trying to get back in the car before Slim came back from inside the store. Slim had no chill what so ever. I got my first glimpse of his split personality one Sunday on MLK in South Dallas. If he would have seen an unknown nigga dressed in rags approaching his vehicle he would have lost it.

It was taking him forever to come back to the car and I became paranoid, looking over my shoulders to make sure he wasn't witnessed me conversing with anyone.

"What's up Larry?" I asked for clarity.

"What are you doing on this side of town?" He questioned.

"Oh, nothing, just passing through headed back to school." I said. "Has everything been ok with you?"

"I've been better, another day in the H, but it was good to see you, Chameleon, you've never looked better," he said with conviction.

I was hoping he would wrap the fucking conversation up, although I did not want to be rude. He was an old friend and all. But the last thing I needed was some unnecessary ass drama between Slim and I.

I could see Larry gathering up his belongings that sat behind the dumpster and he faded off into the darkness of the street lights. The coast was finally clear, shit at least I thought it was. The tension in my body began to lessen a little until I heard some loud commotion coming from inside the gas station.

"What the fuck was taking him so long?" I kept asking myself. I could see the inside of the store from the parking lot. Without being about to completely make out the person standing directly behind Slim in line, I knew those lips from any fucking where.

You had to be fucking kidding me because this could not be life.

"When did he get here...where did he come from?"

"How did I miss him entering the parking lot?"

Fuck that, "how did I miss him entering the fucking store?" I was questioning the fuck out of myself and no one was around to give me any answers.

Empress Hyder

I could still see Larry through the tent of the car and it was then I knew he had something to do with it. He stood across the street motionless looking in the direction of the front of the store with a face of disgust. As if he timed the altercation.

My conscience wanted me to break it up while it was all still just small talk. My gut told me to stay out of it because I knew Slim was dangerous and Lamar was emotional. I had already hurt Lamar enough but to actually see the nigga, who I left him to be with, that would send any nigga into a rant.

The door to the store flew open, I swear that bitch was about to shatter into a million and one pieces and out comes the two of them barking at each other's throat.

"So you're the nigga she's fucking with now?" No other words were uttered after that before I witnessed Lamar plant a smooth jab into Slim's left cheek.

My heart was pounding uncontrollably. *"Calm down bitch,"* I said internally. My legs were shaking like a fucking stripper. Mind racing one hundred miles an hour. I just knew they could see me through the tent. I could feel Slim's eyes piercing through the driver's side window. I had to get out. I had to do and say something. Things were getting physical and Lamar had probably landed himself a death sentence.

"She will never be your bitch," Lamar lashed out at Slim.

"Coming from a nigga who still lives at home with his momma, you ain't nothing but a bitch yourself," Slim replied with a chuckle.

Slim stumbled back trying to break his fall, while wiping the blood from his lip. With his head down he charged Lamar at full speed and pushed him down into the pavement.

"Don't you ever disrespect a grown ass man, little nigga, unlike these other niggas, I will fucking kill you." Slim began to yell in rage.

I couldn't let this go on any longer, so I hopped out the car, you should have seen me trying to bust a move. At full speed I ran towards the two of them who stood in the center of the crowd. I rushed in between the two of them but by this time Lamar had his gun drawn. I never knew him to be that person. I had never seen so much pain in his eyes. We hadn't spoken so I really didn't understand why he was acting out in such a way. I looked left at Lamar who was yelling out for Slim to put his gun away and fight him like a man. Then I looked right at Slim and pleaded for him to put the gun away. The both of them were looking at me like they wanted to know who side I was on.

"You can't have us both, but if you know like I know you better play your cards right?" Slim said, in one of the most life threatening tones I had ever heard.

"How do you choose between the man who was once the love of your life and the man who was turning your dreams into a reality?" My heart wanted to leave with Lamar. I wanted to apologize and make it all right again. My mind and body wanted to get back in the car and go with Slim. Then again my soul wanted none of this to be taking place right now.

Empress Hyder

While I was trying to make a decision, the crowd of people began to increase by the numbers. People had their phones out ready to record the brawl they thought was about to go down. At this point, I had to make a choice and I had to make it quick. *"Why the fuck was I hesitating?"*

It was almost as if I wanted to see them fight myself and maybe that was the problem. Maybe I was the inconsiderate one. *"Who really deserved me and to what extent were they willing to go?"* This situation was escalating before my eyes, but I chose who I chose for my own personal reasons.

I hovered over Slim trying to get his muscular ass arms from around Lamar's neck. "You're going to fucking kill him my nigga," I screamed, traumatized by the look in Lamar's eyes. "What the fuck does it matter to you?" He questioned.

"He's not even fucking worth it, let's go, let's go now," I demanded. You could hear the hurt in my voice. This is not how I wanted them to meet. I wasn't even sure how the fuck Lamar knew who Slim was. I hadn't posted any pictures of us. Lamar and I were not even talking to each other for him to act out the way he did. I was becoming frustrated with the whole situation at hand. My words kept replaying in the back of my head, when I turned to return to the car. *"Did I really just say he wasn't worth it when this nigga was still my everything?"* I really couldn't face the funk but I'd be damn if I left any one of them niggas see that side of me.

"Slim let him go, LET'S FUCKING GO RIGHT NOW." I yelled behind me noticing he was still in full attack mode.

My nerves were shocked and I could feel the anger and frustration building up in my body. This wasn't a coincidence at all, this was merely just bad fucking luck.

I had never seen this nigga like this. I hadn't even given myself time to heal and here I was with some more bullshit on my hand. They both could tell in that moment, from the language of my body and the change in my tone I had no energy for the drama. I didn't give a damn who killed who, but I would soon regret that notion. I was ready to flee the scene, and I didn't give a fuck who was coming with me. Even if it meant him or I were driving the fucking car out of the parking lot.

You could hear the sirens from the police cars coming down the street. They were getting louder so you could tell they were getting closer and we had to leave now. Shit, neither one of us were from around those parts and I was not about to go to jail in Houston behind some niggas fighting over some pussy. Pride. Whatever the fuck the issue may have been. I wasn't going.

I could hear footsteps behind me but I never turned around to see who it was. I knew it would not stop here and this was only the beginning of them coming into contact. By the time I made it back to my side of the car, Slim was crawling into the driver's seat himself.

The mood had completely changed when he put the car in reverse. He was from the hood so you know he knew how to drive a getaway car. There was complete silence. He was looking straight ahead as if he was in the car alone. So I joined him in the motherfucking madness. No nigga was about to make me feel bad. Not Him. Not Lamar. No nigga.

Empress Hyder

    I was trying to rest my leg on the door to stop it from trembling. In this state, I wasn't sure what this nigga was capable of and I didn't want to take any chases. By any means, Ruth taught me how to get a nigga up off of me and with every ounce of blood running through my veins I prayed I wouldn't be pushed to the test.

    "So you are just going to sit over there pretending nothing fucking happened?" the tone of his voice frightened me.

    "What was I supposed to do?" I asked calmly to avoid any static.

    "Have my fucking back, that's what CJ." He shouted.

    "I have never fought over no bitch, and my plans have to start now."

    "Bitch?" I questioned.

    My own friends didn't call me a bitch and I was not going to let any nigga disrespect for that matter. "So now I'm a bitch?" I asked.

    "A bitch Slim, really?" I repeated.

    "Well, you know what you can do for me my nigga take me back to the yard." I stated to end the conversation.

    "Nah, I ain't taking you nowhere blood, but you can get the fuck out of my car, before I drag you out," Slim said with the eyes of Satan as he finally turned his head to make eye contact with me.

    I needed a blunt and I needed it quick. I just knew this nigga hadn't threatened to put me out, yet along drag me if I didn't get out the car myself. So I did what any bitch would do in a hostile environment. I shifted my body and I glanced at my phone for a quick second to find something funny on the web to entertain me.

"You can get the fuck out now," He demanded. I guess he felt I had ignored his statement. It took everything in me not to say something I would only regret in the end. So since he insisted, I reached for the fucking door, while he was coming to a stop. Not only had I regret coming to Houston but before I could even get one foot out of the car, I could feel an uneasy feeling overcoming my body. I could tell then I was in danger. I slowly turned my head, scared to make any sudden movements. I attempted to reach behind me to grab my phone out of my purse, which was sitting in the back sit on the floor directly behind Slim. Shuffling through all the shit I had inside of my purse I could hear Lamar's ringtone.

"Moment of honesty
Someone's gotta take the lead tonight."

By the grace of God himself I made it to my phone just in time to silence the ringer.

"Are you serious?" Slim asked in disgust.

"I have nothing to do with that Slim."

"I can stop a motherfucker from calling my phone."

Before I could even take my eyes off of the text message following Lamar's declined phone call, WHAM.

The next thing I knew Slim punched the dog shit out of me at least three times, right in my face, causing me to fall into the dashboard. My ear was ringing, my face was trembling, and I could feel the blood oozing from my nose. Slim froze, as if he could not believe what he had just done to me. My hair strewn all over my tear-streaked face, he reached over and handed me a Kleenex.

"Clean yourself up." He said.

I just sat there. I had no fight in me. Here I was wondering how I would've reacted if he would have pushed me out the car and his bitch ass just hit me like I was a motherfucking nigga. I literally sat there in shock. I was fucking furious. I just knew someone was about to die today and it was not going to be me.

"Camille?" Slim said, feeling a sense of regret at once. He pulled off onto a side street and got out the car rushing over to the passenger side. He bent down to help me up, as if I needed his assistance, but I pushed him away with all of the strength in my right arm. My eyes filled with defiance, I rose from the dashboard and with my purse slung over my shoulder I took off running as fast as I could. I felt the dust kick up from my shoes and when Slim went to grab me, adrenaline kicked in. I had to get the fuck away from him and I had to do it fast.

Unaware of where I was and what part of town I was in, I just kept running until my lungs felt like they were going to collapse. Crying and running, I managed to come to a gas station in a well lite area.

Slim couldn't have been too far away, because as I was running, from behind me I could hear the roaring from his engine coming in my direction. *"I couldn't believe this nigga hit me like I was one of his old hoes."*

You should have seen me running for my life and reaching for my phone. *"Who could I call?"* I couldn't get in touch with anyone and I needed someone to come to my rescue, and to make it to me as fast as they could before Slim found me and killed me.

    I rushed passed the cashier who was approaching the door to shut down for the night. Ran into the bathroom damn near knocking the store's janitor into the wall. I locked the door behind me that way no one could enter. Approaching the mirror I was nervous to see the damage done to my face.

    I removed a light jacket from out of my purse and placed the hood upon my head to hide whatever damage had been done.

    "I couldn't wait to tell Dookie this shit." Slim had just started a war and he didn't even know it yet. I knew if anyone was waiting for a moment to go to war with Slim it would be my brother.

    With my head held down ashamed of my appearance and my hands tucked into my pockets I powered walk towards the door. If you were a customer in the store you would have sworn I was either up to no good or stealing.

    Shortly after exiting the store from buying a bottled Big Red, I heard the engine of a car pull up in front of me. I froze dead in my steps. My feet were planted firmly into the ground, my back was stiff as a board and my hands were shaking irrepressibly. I was hesitant to look and see who it was. I even jumped as the voice that called out, "Camille."

    Although I recognized that voice from anywhere, the way he said my name still sent chills down my spine. My heart dropped. Not in a bad way but in a state of relief. When I arose my head to look up from underneath my hood to make sure it was who I thought it was, it was my knight in shining armor. Not wanting to believe that for once he was in the right place at the right time a feeling of comfort came over my body. *"How the fuck did he find me?"*

Here I was running for my life not knowing what the fuck Slim was capable of, with nowhere to go. And, yet again, there Lamar was coming to my rescue.

"So are you coming with me?" Lamar questioned with sincerity in his eyes.

"I guess so, shit I don't have anywhere else to go...look at me." I replied in disbelief to what had just happened.

With my hood gripped tight around my face, trying to cover my eye and my purse tucked tight underneath my arm, I crawled into the passenger seat. *"See this was exactly why I loved this man."*

All I had was $250 to my name. I had no clothes and no ride back to the yard for the night but I knew Lamar would take me if I needed him to do so. And I was not in any rush to leave his presence or rush back to my car where this nigga may have been waiting.

Like clockwork, calls from Renay and Slim were both blowing up my cellphone back to back. Back to back. Back to back. I had grown annoyed to sound of that bitch ringing so I furiously put my phone on silent in attempt to enjoy the rest of my night.

Silence.

That was exactly what the fuck I needed.

Silence and a fucking ice pack.

"So are you going to let me know why you haven't looked my way?" Lamar asked with concern.

"I......I just, I don't want to talk about it, just get me away from here." I could feel him staring at me. If anyone knew when something was wrong with me, Lamar knew for sure. He didn't put up a fight, he simply just let it be. He turned the volume up to 15 and we just rode through the city streets like old times.

You should've seen the way my body responded knowing I was safe. You could by the limpness in my physique, mind and soul that I was out of harm's way. Shit, at least for the night.

"Slow Loud and Bangin', all in my trunk. Trunk full of funk, I ain't never been a punk. I blow on skunk, I blow on doja. Military minded, I'm a motherfucking soldier..."

Mo City Don by Z-Ro filled the car and I instantly tapped into the chick from the Pleasant Grove. Rapping along with the lyrics and grooving to the music, Slim was the last thing on my mind.

And I'm gone, nigga old glory
I'm H-Town to Cali, just like Robert Ory
If I do a murder, flee the murder scene
No missing shortage on the drank, I can't find no lean.

Lamar knew just how to get me to snap out of whatever mood I was in. I knew when he went scrolling through his play list he would start reminiscing on how shit use to be.

ALL OF A SUDDEN THE MUSIC STOPPED. I'm talking mid-fucking rap stopped. Right in the middle of my favorite verse. I was in my zone, pointing my fingers, bobbing my head, saying every verse without missing a beat. The whole nine and then some. I was in performance mode.

"What the fuck happened to your face?" Lamar asked demanding an answer.

"Huh" I responded with this confused look on my face as if I didn't understand why he would ask some shit like that.

"Nothing, Lamar, there you go over exaggerating shit."

"Ok, Camille."

"He didn't mean to hit me that hard."

"Right on, Camille."

"He didn't mean to hit me at all, but you wouldn't stop fucking calling." I yelled out in frustration.
"So this is my fault, right Camille?"
"So this is the type of shit you like, maybe I should've knocked your ass out a few times then huh?" Lamar yelled. By the attitude in his voice I could tell he was even more pissed than when he initially saw my face. But threaten me didn't make the shit any better. Before I would let this nigga antagonize me, I would walk the fuck back to Prairie View.

I was tired of arguing and really could have cared less how the night ended so I asked Lamar to take me back to the yard. In which his bitch as refused because you already know his plan was to try to make shit right once again.

Sadly, I really didn't want to be alone tonight. The bruise on my face made me want to stay, but the ring on my finger made me want to go.

Lamar wasn't going to let me leave his sight. At least not in the state I was in. There were only two things that would get my mind right, some liquor and some dick. With the mood I was in and the vibe I was feeling myself after a few shots of my favorite cognac. Lamar was about to be my sex slave and slim was about to be my victim.

Slim- "Meet me at 3505 Sage, Rd, Houston TX 77056."

Slim- "I'm sorry and I really need to see you."

Slim- "Call me."

Slim- "Door number 214"

I could see all of his text messages coming through but I had no sense of urgency to reply. Slim knew he had fucked up. He knew I was nothing like those other bitches he was use to controlling. By then I was sure he had recognized he would have to work just as hard to get me back than he did to initially get me. Shit, all I could do was stare at my phone in disgust. I knew he didn't think he could go upside my head and in a matter of hours everything would be ok.

Growing up niggas only threaten to hit me and never did. But he executed the motherfucking thought and made a liar out of me and he needed to deal with the consequences of his actions. I bet like hell he would never hit anyone else.

"You first." Lamar said with a grin as he led me outside the door of the restaurant.

'Thank You..., thank you for everything." I said in a slur.

I wanted to launch my engagement ring across the damn parking lot of Chaco's, but pawning it would've been more rewarding.

I could feel my body temperature rising. Those Hennessey shots were settling into my blood stream. Fuck

Empress Hyder

being loose as a goose, I was trying to get Lamar to take me home. No lie, I missed him and I knew he missed me and I also knew he could read my mind. He knew exactly how far I would go if he got me in the right mood. If any nigga knew the maze to my soul, it was definitely him.

So I walked up to Lamar and sat my ass on his dick to see if I still had it. The way I was feeling he could have gotten it all plus some in the parking lot.

"You better stop playing before I start reminiscing." Lamar whispered in my ear. He grabbed a hand full of my ass and then spun me around and kissed my neck. A kiss on the neck led to a kiss on the cheek. A kiss on the cheek led to my legs pushed above my head once we made it back to his house.

Lamar stroked my cheeks and kissed my lips. Our lips moved in time with each other. He knew exactly what I liked. From neck grapping to lip and tongue sucking. It was like a scene out of a porno on xxvideos.com. Lamar raised his hands up to my hair and tangled his fingers in it. He cupped my cheek with his other hand. I began raising up his shirt so that I could feel his body pressed against mine.

I moved from his lips to his neck thrusting myself onto his thighs. I was in a total daze but all I cared about was how good it felt to be in his presence and how good he was about to fuck my brains out.

"I-Love-You," panted Lamar through the hard kissing, fucking and touching. My hands came up and grasped his biceps firmly, pushing up his sleeve as my tongue lapped at the insides of his elbow. I began to make soft mewling sounds and he locked eyes with me and just watched. Lamar eyes wide unable to pull back from me and it was like our souls were interlocking. His erection feeling huge and uncomfortable between my legs, he began to thrust harder and harder at a very fast pace. His mouth was filling with saliva but before he swallowed compulsively, licking his lips, he pulled his manhood out of me and trickled his way down to my pussy that was dripping with sweet essences.

I was waiting for this moment to quench his thirst because Lamar would suck me dry, until I had nothing else to give. And, that was exactly what I needed. I gripped the crown of his head, lifted my legs and shoved his face in it. I knew he could feel my pussy throbbing. Not to get off topic but I can feel my shit throbbing now just thinking about. Anyway, he sucked on my clit as if he were drinking from it. This was the most pure sensation of our lives together, and my thoughts, my building guilt and burning questioning mind were silenced in the wave of pleasure rising touching every nerve.

THE FESTIVITIES WERE COMING TO AN END and I couldn't stop thinking about him. But I was not hurting anymore. I did not want him anymore. I did not hate him and the craving I had for his presence had finally been satisfied.

That night was definitely a night to remember. Casual fun just the way I liked it. Not to mention, being with him was everything I desired and needed at the time. Everything about our encounter was faultless, well at least the last half was. It was exactly what I needed to get my head back in the zone to remember who the fuck I was. I was a gift to these niggas and if a man couldn't respect me then he didn't deserve me. I hadn't lost my balance yet and I wasn't about to lose it. Then again the game was to be played to win not to surrender and there was nothing that would eat away at a nigga pride more than another nigga fucking his main bitch.

    I woke up at the crack of dawn to sound of his damn alarm. My hair tied, oversized shirt and my favorite lace panties. It was 6:35 in the morning and time for me to head back to my car only to make a turnaround trip. My head had just touched down on our pillows not even three hours ago and it was time to start the day. Only the lord and my hormones knew where I had been on that late night and early morning. All he knew was that Renay contacted me for some last minute drinks being that she was on this side of town entertaining somebody's man as always.

    "Camille are you up, baby?" Slim asked from the open bathroom door. It's crazy how after a night of getting piped down by Lamar I ended up right back under Slim.

    "I just want to," I stopped him before he could another word.

    "You weren't sorry when you did it, so no need to apologize Ethan." I replied, you could hear a pen drop in the room. Everything around us froze as we just stood there staring at each other.

    I was hung over. My head was hurting so badly I could hardly lift it off the pillow. The sun was peeking through the blinds creating a glare from the mirror on the wall. And Slim was hovering over me waiting for his apology to be accepted like a disobedient ass puppy.

"Damn, you must've have one hell of a night with cha girl," I heard Slim say under his breathe.

"Get out," I groaned. I could hear him fumbling through the closest purposely trying to irritate the hell out of me.

"Slim, could you please get the fuck out." I requested.

I tried opening my eyes completely, one at a time to see if my energy level would shift. It didn't. So I figured I would lay still for at least 15 more minutes until I could move without regurgitating.

"Everything okay?" Slim asked. I guess he decided to ignore the fact that I wanted him out my sight.

"Everything is great Slim, I answered as I grabbed the pillow next to me and placed it over my face.

"Get out, please." I yelled from underneath my duvet. I could hear Slim whispering on the phone as he slammed the room door behind him. The doorbell rang and no one knew I was here so who the fuck was at the door this early in the morning. For starters Slim would never do business out of his place of residence. Nor would he let his potnas stop by and I was present. He wasn't the type of nigga to mix business with pleasure so you know I made my way to the door.

"So you must have company?" a female's voice inquired from outside the door. But the way Slim had his body positioned I couldn't see anything but her legs. I waited around the corner for her to say something else before I jumped to conclusions. I was almost certain Slim heard the bedroom door creep open which is why he was pretending it was someone ringing the wrong doorbell.

"Who was that?" I asked from the hallway.

"Why? It wasn't for you." He replied as if I were going to drop the subject.

"Oh really, so a bitch can pop up at my house and I get told it wasn't for me."

"You never cease to amaze me." I responded. "You, Ethan, you never cease to fucking amaze me" I repeated at least three more times to get my point across.

A few minutes later, the doorbell rang again. So I politely shoot passed Slim to get to the door first.

"Can I help you?" I asked as I quickly pulled the door open. Shocked by the person who stood on the other side, our eyes met and her body stiffened.

"Renay?" I prayed I was being punked. I can't even began to describe the look that came across my face that day.

"Are you ready to go?" she asked.

Knowing I wasn't with this bitch at all last night, I hadn't tapped into what the fuck was going on. Somebody was about to get their ass whooped and it wasn't going to be me. I knew this nigga had the trifling nigga syndrome but it was too damn early in the game to be pulling these kind of stunts.

I did what any female would have done in my case, I went along with the flow. I had no proof that anything was going on between them so I didn't get too beside myself. Plus I needed a ride back to the yard and she obviously was at my service.

"How did you know I was here?" I asked curiously, especially being a few minutes before she showed up, there was a bitch at the door questioning my nigga about who was inside. Hence, the apartment he got for me. Hell this wasn't even his shit and it wasn't about to be ours. That was not what was discussed.

"Girl, you texted me last night and told me you needed a ride back to the yard". She replied. "I'll be in the car, but hurry up." she added before getting on the elevator.

Slim was in the kitchen pretending to be fixing him something to drank, so I hurried passed him to grab my things and headed out the door.

Without making any attempt to walk me out, he uttered, "I love you."

"I'll call you when I make," I retorted before closing the door behind me. You should've seen how the wall shook from the force of slamming that door as I made my exit. I was in a fuck love state and he was in for a rude awaken from that day forward.

I was never known to play the game raw but my attitude was slaw and I was ready to go to war with him and whoever else. The crazy thing about the whole situation as I approached the door to Renay's car, I didn't remember texting anyone that night, but the outgoing messages in my phone said differently.

I guess I was more intoxicated than I realized.

June 16th, 2015

"I never saw a wild thing sorry for itself. A small bird will drop frozen dead from a bough without ever having felt sorry for itself."

-D.H. Lawrence

Empress Hyder

◆ ◆ ◆

You have to forgive me for the delay but I had to step away from the computer screen writing this lovely tell all story for you as I tended to the twins. "Good morning Miss Jones," the front desk clerk whispered as I approached the front desk. Noticing my face was buried in my phone, she proceeded to handing me my favorite pen to sign-in.

"Good morning, I replied rudely without even pulling my eyes from the screen. Our exchange of words were nothing new. Neither one of us took anything personal, that's just the way it had been since the scheduling of these morning appointments. A morning person was something I wasn't and these weekly doctor visits are starting to kick my ass. You would think having an appointment would mean you would at least be seen on time. I was paying all of this money, $844 per visit for my Ob/Gyn to ask me if I had any questions for her. It was the same thing every time. Sitting in a waiting room full of fertile bitches for at least forty-five minutes to an hour only to be finally seen for ten minutes tops.

"Camille," Susey, the nurse practitioner called from behind the ajar door.

"How are you?" she asked, as if my answer ever changed.

"Ready to have these babies," I replied.

"Only a few weeks left, you can do it." she replied with excitement in her voice.

It's almost as if you are visiting with me. Patiently waiting in Room 3 for my Ob to walk in with hopefully news of taking the twins tomorrow. I'm beyond tired and in all honesty I'm really just ready to see my babies. To keep my anxiety down I try to write as much as I can with the time I have especially while sitting in the waiting room waiting to be seen. Or even taking breaks throughout the day to bring The Tell All of Camille Jones to an end. There is so much more you guys are about to find out and if I could stay off of social media long enough, this book would probably be finished. I've literally taking this thing day by day and it hasn't been easy.

Between making sure the twins have everything they need for their arrival. Unpacking all of their gifts from their baby shower and adjusting to living with Lamar all over again. Finally, life is better. It's not exactly where I want to be, but I know I'm headed in the right direction.

It was told to me it was rare that a woman could carry two healthy baby girls almost full term without any complications. By means of trying to keep the stress level down and dealing with hate messages from catfish bitches wishing I would miscarriage, I have only four and a half weeks to go. Originally due to deliver the twins in September I am scheduled to have them arrive July 9th.

In between preparing for their arrival here I am reminiscing trying to keep you guys engaged on what the fuck really happened during this love triangle. I'm supposed to be resting and nesting but this story isn't going to write itself. Sometimes it's hard to find the words to say. It's hard to tell this shit without caring about what other people think

Empress Hyder

but at this point, I'm in too deep and I just know you are dying to know what happened after Renay dropped me back off to my car at the MSC.

There was disloyalty, dishonesty, and weeping would consume my life the next few days and months to come. Betrayal and deception became a lifestyle. Deceit became my last name.

Only the strongest really survived but who knew that would literally be me in the end.

Chapter Nine

Empress Hyder

"I'd spent so long trying to fit in, trying to be someone I wasn't, that I had no idea who I was any more."

— Dorothy Koomson, *The Rose Petal Beach*

Wrapping up a conversation with Renay was almost impossible. "Alright girl, I'll call you later," I shouted from the window as I pulled out the parking lot of the MSC. I got all the way back to my new part of town only to make the same trip tomorrow morning. And every other day after that.

As soon as I got to the front door of my condo, I could hear commotion seeping through the cracks. Only to find Slim and his potnas watching football highlights like I didn't have class in the morning. I was already frustrated so the last thing I wanted was some fucking company that didn't belong to me. Random niggas for that matter.

I couldn't even have peace in my own shit and I'm usually cool about him having company on the days he would visit, but not today.

"Say yo boys gotta go," I said staring him dead in his face.

"NOW." I screeched to the top of my lungs.

He knew I was not in the mood and I did not want to be bothered by him nor three other niggas I didn't even know. Not to mention in the back of my mind, I still had some curiosity as to how Renay knew where I was. She knew the exact location but I was going to let that shit slide for the time being.

Empress Hyder

"Ma, don't start tripping." He chuckled, acting as if he ran shit. As if everything was cool, when the only person relaxed in the room was him.

"Slim, you said this was my condo, and I don't want them in my shit."

"Ya'll can leave out the same door ya'll came in." I yelled.

"Aghhhh it's like that ma," an unfamiliar voice asked.

"Yes, that's exactly how it is, and you are?" I questioned as if I were interested in knowing.

Slim immediately interrupted, that's my boy Cesar, that's Cass and that's, pointing to guy seating on the floor rolling a blunt, is my little brother Rook. You should've seen the look on my face when Rook picked his head up and gave me his undivided attention to say hello.

"What's up?" He nodded and returned to seal his cigarillo.

He was the politest young man, in Slim's circle and the only motherfucker to speak. I knew he too had a killer in him that was not to be disturbed. So I headed towards the kitchen hoping they would be gone by the time the microwave dinged.

Politely grabbing his car keys, strap and phone from the armrest of the love seat, Slim got up without putting up a fuss. He got his shit and his boys and they went on their way.

"Answer the phone when I call." He said before closing the door behind him and his three man entourage.

With no response, I charged towards the front door to make sure it was locked. Knowing he had a key, I had to take action fast. There was no telling what he was thinking after the incident in the car and I was not trying to find out.

Knock. Knock.

I dared not to make any sudden movement thinking whoever was on the other side of the door could hear any step I took.

Knock. Knock. Knock

The knocks got harder. There was no way to even see who it could be. Ironically, these expensive ass apartments didn't even have a damn peep hole. They were asking for residents to receive uninvited guest.

"Camille" someone called from outside. From the voice I knew it wasn't Slim.

Knock. Knock. Knock

I put my right hand on the door and the knocks stopped. I unbolted the dead bolt and proceeded to open to door to find no one there. I noticed someone approaching the elevator so I called out to them.

"Can I help you?" I asked.

"Oh damn, well yes you can." He replied softly.

Before stepping a foot into the door he informed me he had left his phone inside. "Do you mind getting it for me?" He asked graciously. His voice. Those eyes. I hadn't noticed them before because Slim would've murdered the both of us on sight if he became suspicious of anything.

"Rook is it?" I asked to reassure that was the name Slim gave me. "Rook the cookie crook that's me," He stated jokingly.

"Come in." I insisted.

Empress Hyder

     I did a pivot turn in the foyer of the apartment and I could feel him staring at me, but I didn't want any problems. "Is this it?" I inquired picking up an iPhone off of the floor in the same spot he was sitting in before he left. I knew it was but I just wanted to make conversation. I didn't want to keep him to long knowing Slim was in the parking garage waiting. So I made the exchange rapidly.

     "Yea ma, that's it." He replied with a slight head nod.

     "Thank you!" was the last thing he said as he slowly took his phone out of my hand. Those 5 seconds were golden but I didn't think neither one of us were bold enough to cross Slim. Oh but the thought was definitely one that crossed my mind.

     As I walked over to close the door behind him. I could feel the butterflies. The same butterflies I felt when I first came face to face with Slim. I pushed my body into the door and slid to the floor. Knowing I could have him, I wanted to see if it were mutual. All of this was too close for comfort but I was in for the ride and up for a new challenge.

     That deadbolt would come in handy for the time being, because as long as I was home alone I didn't have to worry about anyone coming over unannounced. I didn't have to worry about getting caught either.

     It was still early so I had plenty of time to unload my clothes from the car, wash, shower and relax before entering into a new semester tomorrow. Second semester of my sophomore year and being off campus would give me a whole new focus. I was taking 18 hours and it was completely grind time. My classes would include: ECON 2123 Macroeconomics, HIST 1323 The U.S. – 1876 to

Present, MATH 1153 Finite Math, PSYC 1113 General Psychology, MGMT 2203 Leadership and Ethics, and MGMT 1163 Quantitative Business Analysis. This workload was nothing I could not handle but I was determined to graduate with a 4.0 so it was about to get real. I hadn't got this far in life by slacking, and failing was just merely not an option.

The only thing I dreaded about being on campus for the duration of my class periods was the likelihood of running into Lamar. Even though he was an agriculture major, we shared some of the same friends and the Memorial Student Center was the hang out for all students, especially on Wednesdays.

Monday, Wednesday and Fridays I would take four classes and be done by noon. Tuesday and Thursday I would take the remaining two courses and be done by 2:00 P.M. Though I loved my new schedule for this semester I was not a morning person. Making that drive from Houston to Prairie View which is already an hour within itself would get old quick. At least after the first month it did.

With the semester in progress Slim would come into town and leave out of town as he pleased and I preferred it to be that way. Not only had things picked up for him in the streets but he began to use his supply more than normal. Different sides of him began to show. The sides that I've heard about and the side that came out the night we were in Houston. Everything about him became aggressive and abusive. He would fuck me when he wanted to and beat me when he had a bad day. If he came up short I was blamed. If I came home late because of traffic that resulted in a fight. God forbid I denied him sex, chances are I would get pistol whipped in the ribs and forced to perform. He even raped me once on my period.

Slim was a strategic abuser. He would damage everything but the face because he knew then it was easier to get away with it. There would be nights I would crash on campus after meetings and study sessions and of course he eventually became suspicious. He knew my entire schedule and if he hadn't heard from me immediately after class it would be a fight when I got home.

It was the second month into school and here we were making our first Valentine's Day plans only for shit to go downhill. I remember texting him to get an idea of what he wanted to do and his replies were so dry they began to raise a red flag. It was Friday, February 11, 2011 and I was anxious to see what my future husband had in store for me.

On my way home after class I decided to grab some panda express and text Slim for our weekend plans.

Me: You know Valentine's Day falls on a Monday so you what do you want to do?

Slim: Whatever you want to do.

Slim: Why don't you just cook for a nigga, we don't have to go out.

Me: I'll come up with something, but I'm not really in for staying in.

Slim: I'll let you know

Slim: Me and my bro may have to make some runs

Me: OK, meet me at the house.

We barely spent time together as it was and now all of a sudden he wanted to stay in as if I was his side bitch or something. As if he was hiding me from something and/or someone.

Pulling into the parking garage I noticed my favorite spot had been taken and I had entirely too much shit to transport from my car to my front door to park in the back. I guess this day was my lucky day because as this olive Honda Accord pulled out of the parking spot near the elevator I shifted my gear into reverse and got right in it. Without getting a good look at the driver I could have sworn it was Renay, but why would she be on my side of town this time of night.

"You need some help with that?" a familiar voice asked from a distance. Fumbling to put all of my belonging in my purse and grabbing my books out the back seat I had too much going on before noticing he had already approached the trunk of my car.

"Rook?"

"Surprised to see me?" he asked while grabbing my books from underneath my arm.

He powered walked in front of me to make sure we didn't have to wait on the elevator, because sometimes it worked and sometimes it didn't. All that damn money was being spent and I didn't have a damn peep hole and would be stranded outside waiting on the elevator every other night.

"Are you alone?" I asked wondering why he was here.

"For now, ya boy said he was on his way."

The elevator ride was quiet. It made me a little nervous to be alone with him especially with suspicions of being setup.

Empress Hyder

So I kept my cool and my distance. Once we got inside, I gave him notice that I was about to get in the shower. My typical routine before cooking and studying.

"Could you let your brother in when he gets here?" I shouted from my bedroom.

I undressed as if I had an audience watching. I loved everything about my body when it was bruised. Happily the bruise underneath my right rib was disappearing.

Nonetheless, it had been at least a week since I had been touched due to fucking Mother Nature.

The first drop of water touched my skin releasing all of the pressure in my shoulders I had built up. I began to sing as always and then there was a knock on the door.

"*Did I lock the door?*" I began to ask myself.

Knock. Knock. Knock. The knocks were really light but thinking it was Slim I gave them the right away to come in.

The steam had the entire bathroom foggy and no one was recognizable unless they were standing directly in front of me. The door to my glass standup shower flew open and there stood Rook with nothing but his Nike slides on and his dick in his hand.

He stepped inside and eased the door shut.

"What about Slim?" I stuttered.

"What about him?" He replied back.

"I told him you may have not made it home yet." He continued.

Why he would say something like that knowing sooner than later Slim would be ringing my phone, I had the slightest idea. Being the both of us seemed unbothered, I dropped my head so the water could touch the back of my neck before running down my spine. Rook began to trickle his finger around each curve on my body until he got around to my clit. He pulled me into him by my waist like a snake slithering around their prey purposely placing his dick between my ass cheeks. I turned around with my eyes closed pressing my lips up against his soft skin. The water squelched between our bodies causing this passionate aura coming from one another filling the atmosphere around us.

"Rook." I whimpered as his body pushed mine until I was between him and the glass wall of the shower. The icy feeling from the wall sent goosebumps all over my body causing the moment to pause for a brief second. He hadn't said a word. Completely in his zone he grabbed my arms pushing them up against the wall, his fingers locking with mine. He leaned in and kissed all around my face; my nose, my cheek, my forehead until finally reaching my lips. He pushed himself forward, lifting me up by my waist; his body began to tense as my body began to melt from our first momentous sexual connection. The electrifying pleasure pulsing through my body caused me to let out a slightly louder cry then normal.

"We can't do this." I whispered in his ear as I gripped his back.

"If you want me to stop I will." He replied making sure he had direct eye contact with me.

The sounds from my vocal cords escaping my mouth as he repeatedly pushed himself inside of me was the climax I needed. Our breath fell heavy as the sweat from our bodies blended with the water that fell from above; our gaze meeting as we rested upon each other's forehead, giggling and staring with love and nuzzling noses in the last moments of our first of many passionate hours.

The vibe changed in the atmosphere. Someone was in my apartment. I could feel their presence when we got out of the shower. There was something different from when we came in an hour ago. I could hear the noise from the TV coming through the walls. But when I heard a noise coming from my guest bedroom, I started to get a little scared.

"Rook, did you leave the TV on?" I asked him trying to stop my body from trembling from the breeze coming through the vents.

"I might have left it on, but I'll go check it out."

"You stay here," he added, taking on the role of my protector. *"What if it were Slim, what would we tell him?"* I didn't want to face death today and if Slim found out I were fucking his brother, I would be unrecognizable in my casket.

"Wait," I said stopping him before opening the door so that I could get dressed.
He reached for the door while pulling up his pants and you would not believe who was coming down the hallway towards us. My heart began to pound. *"What the hell?"*

I was almost floored when I saw Lamar standing in front of us. Everything in me wanted to run and jump into his arms, but with the look he and Rook were giving each other, I refused to witness another fight.

"What are you doing here, I haven't heard from you in a month." I asked in a low-pitched tone.

"Exactly you ain't shit," he said as he approached me in attempt to give me a kiss.

"Did I interrupt something?" he asked with a grin on his face.

"Actually, I was just leaving, ya'll enjoy your night." Rook replied before hugging me tight and gripping a handful of my ass.

I could tell he was getting under Lamar skin, so I suggested he let me walk him out, in case he had something to get off his chest.

"Aye ma, hit me up later." Rook said as he made his grand exit. After we said our goodbyes and I went back inside to deal with Lamar. Everything about him was just too tranquil. I didn't mind but it kind of had me on the edge.

"I can't believe you're here. What happened? You know what I don't care, I'm just glad to see your face." I grabbed his hand and led him back into the living.

"Lamar you can't be here, even as bad as I want you to stay." I told him with my head down.

"I wanted to surprise you." He chimed in.

We sat on the sofa and I said, "I know you've been avoiding me on campus."

"Why would you think that, I was just giving you your distance?" He said with a look of concern on his face.

"Camille, are you ok." He asked.

"I'm fine, why would you ask something like that."

"You just don't seem like yourself, but if you say you're ok, I'll take your word for it."
And he dropped the conversation and switched his attention to the television to watch Martin. I excused myself to grab my cellphone off of the charger in my bedroom and not one

missed phone call or text message from Slim. Something didn't feel right about that at all. So I hit his line.

Ring. Ring.

Ring. Ring. Ring.

"Your call has been forwarded to an automated voice messaging system."

He never let his phone die and he never went without checking in on me but nothing at this point in our relationship surprised. It was a different from Dallas. He knew I had no family here and I depended on him for the majority of everything. What he didn't know was that all the extra money he would throw my way was being deposited into a separate account. It was only a matter of time I would have to take my life back and part ways.

I looked into Lamar's face and tried to read his mind but I got nothing. I didn't want to say the wrong thing. I wanted to say the right thing but didn't know the right thing to say.

"I don't….I don't know if you should be here," I said, slightly shrugging my shoulders.

"Things are already a little heated around here and I really think you should go."

"So what do you want to do Camille?" He yelled as he stood up from sitting on the sofa.

"Lamar, keep your voice down." I whispered.

"I want you, Lamar. I've always wanted nothing but you. For us to be happy but you fucked that up for us a long time ago. So why are you really here?"

My phone rang and I was somewhat relieved. When I went to answer it was Rook. I hadn't given him my number so I was confused as to why his name showed up on my caller id. He was slicker than I thought but I kind of liked that about him.

"Hello," I answered on the third ring.

"What's up, CJ." It was Slim's voice coming through the other end of the phone. This motherfucker always had the nerve to call me from other people's phones as if he didn't have his own. Two for that matter, one for personal business and another from the money that was coming in.

"I'm not disturbing you, am I?" He asked but I could tell he was being sarcastic.

"No, Slim. I'm not doing anything at all."

"So you didn't see me calling your phone?" I asked him demanding an answer.

The time it took him to respond I knew that he was about to lie, but I charged it to the game before he even opened up his mouth to reply.

"Never mind, don't even worry about it." I said before hanging up the phone. At the rate we were going we weren't going to make it to the altar. There was no point in planning a wedding for a nigga who was temporary.

I hadn't even noticed that Lamar let himself out without saying a word. Finally I was alone to soak in my own emotional filth. Time was flying and it was already 2:00 o'clock in the morning. Luckily two of my classes were cancelled so I would be done with class by 9:00 A.M. I turned on my Trey Songz station on Pandora and called it a night.

My alarm hadn't gone off just yet but my body knew it was time to wake up and hit the freeway. My eyes squint

Empress Hyder

shut trying to ward off the filtered sunlight drifting through the blind. I jumped out of bed and brushed my teeth. I threw on my favorite pair of distressed blue jeans, a black tank top with no bra, some black combat boots with the shoe strings halfway laced and grabbed my Kate spade tote. It was Friday so all I needed was a spiral and a pen to take notes. Pulled my hair back in a ponytail, applied some lipstick to my lips, placed my shades over my face and headed to my car.

    I made it all the way to the car and realized I had forgotten my phone. *"Fuck my life."* I hurried back to the elevator knowing time was not on my side. My 8:00 A. M. professor was a little bitch and would lock the door if you didn't arrive on time, so I knew I had to get moving. Approaching my door I could see my door was cracked and someone talking from inside. I was not for this bullshit, barely here a month and I just knew I wasn't being robbed. I quietly pushed open the door, making just enough room for me to walk in only to find a video playing on my living room TV. The noise was coming from the surround sound system but being I was in a rush I paid it no mind. I ran to get my phone from off of the charger where I left it. Everything was still intact so I left it at that.

    By the time I made it to the parking garage it was already 7:20 in the morning. Houston traffic was hell, and I knew from experience I wouldn't make it on campus by 8:00 but I tested my luck anyway. Flying down 290 I noticed a blacked impala in my rear view mirror tailing me it seemed. But what the fuck did I have to worry about. I didn't have anyone after me that I knew of so I turned up my volume to 38 and dashed through traffic to get to my destination.

    For the next two weeks or so I would soon notice that the same blacked out impala was always in the same proximity as my car no matter where I would be. On campus, pulling into the parking garage at my apartment, headed out, no matter the time or place. I was being watched. Literally, everywhere I went that was not inside of a building, was not safe for me. I knew then Slim had something to do with this. All of those trips out of town, there was no way he would leave me completely alone. He wanted to know my every move. When arrived to my destination. What time I left. Who I was with. What I had on. Hell he might as well should have had control over my breathing.

    Slim would probably stay the night with me two days out of week and blame the rest on being busy, heading out of town or meeting his Mexican potna. It wasn't until I would find clothing inside of my apartment that didn't belong to me and restaurant receipts for two in his pocket that I began to accuse of him things.

    I knew then if he could look me dead in my face about a shirt that was not my taste of my size, he would look me dead in my face and lie to me about anything.

Chapter Ten

"There is no fulfillment that is not made sweeter for the prolonging of desire"

— Jacqueline Carey

Empress Hyder

◆ ◆ ◆

Every time I wanted to walk away he would constantly ask what he had to do to keep me in his life. Slim would send me text messages like; "So that how it is?" As if he was the victim. Everything about this man had become destructive and manipulative.

"I think I deserve a second chance." As if he hadn't been giving one too many already. The lyrics to "Love is blind" by Eve began to play over and over again in my mind.

"How would you feel if she held you down and raped you?
Tried and tried, but she never could escape you
She was in love and I'd ask her how? I mean why?
What kind of love from a nigga would black your eye?
What kind of love from a nigga every night make you cry?
What kind of love from a nigga make you wish he would die?"

Through the abuse, the threats and multiple visits to the ER I never left his side. Love really was blind and I needed to elevate and find myself. I knew I was only fooling and hurting myself. Knowing I was only relevant when it was convenient. Understanding that even as his fiancé, the person he saw fit to be his future wife, a toxic relationship is what became of us. He wasn't really the type to indulge in a phone conversation so it was easier to express himself through text messages. Again, I settled.

    Slim- *"I really want us to be together Cam, that's why I keep calling baby."*

    Slim- *"Just know I love you Cam with all my heart and I'm willing to spend the rest of my life with you."* You would think he would have gotten the point by then. The fact that I needed my fucking space. Room to think and possibly plan my escape. In came a third text at 1:09 A.M., *"Goodnight Cam, you mean the world to me."*

    One thing I would never understand was why would any of that matter now after all the times I kept trying to keep us together no matter what. He didn't want me, he wanted every other bitch that was going to let him be in full control. Even after I accepted the fact he had gotten her pregnant first three weeks into fucking with her. Then to top that the bitch would let me sleep over at her apartment when I didn't have the energy to make that hour drive knowing she was fucking my nigga. She had my scheduled memorized. And he was supposed to love me.

    In came a forth text at 1:12 A.M., *"I fucked up."* Right hand to the man he had did that a long time ago. We were still supposed to be on good terms this last time around but obviously I wasn't for him because he just couldn't get his shit together. I tried over and over again to figure it out but I couldn't because as soon as I took him back, we would go steady for a month and then be right back to the same old bullshit.

    All of these roads began to become too familiar. We had been down them so many times in such a short period, especially when he began pushing work heavily in Houston. When he couldn't handle the shit he dished out to me he instantly became ready to commit to me.

"Why the fuck did any of those bitches have to come in between us?" They ruined everything. He ruined everything; what we had, what we built, what he let them destroy. For once I wanted him to put himself in my shoes and love a person with all of his being a second time around, and then one day they wake up and feel like you don't even deserve half of them.

Then there was the fifth text at 1:21 A.M., "*I hope you are resting well, we will talk tomorrow I love you.*" Followed by a sixth text at 1:22 A.M.," *I told you I fucked up baby, that's all I can say.*"

All of those fucking text messages but not one apologize. My ass was not even good enough for one genuine ass apology.

I wanted us to be together, but the unstableness was beginning to take a toll on me. I needed to get away for a few days, so I packed up, and planned an impromptu trip to Destin, Florida with my girls back at home for Spring Break. That one week get away was everything and more. We left out on Friday March 11th and returned on Friday March 18th. Tasha, Asia and Tae were the only real friends I had left. My bitches since the very beginning and I was still an angel in their eyes no matter how many flaws I possessed. We would go to bat for each other and it was nothing like being surrounded by people who enjoyed your company over shots of patron for a week with no bullshit.

Tae was a true bad ass yellow bone. The definition of a true friend, who has stayed down with me since Kindergarten at John Quincy Adams Elementary School. She was a half-breed mixed with Mexican and Black. Natural thick hair to the middle of her back and hips wider than all outdoors. She stood about five foot seven, one-hundred-forty-five pounds and was severally pigeon toed but niggas loved that shit. Family-oriented and drowning in cash money. Her blood line ran deep. A mother to my beautiful god daughter and pregnant with her second child. She had just entered into her career as an RN and was doing the damn thing. Tae had only dated two niggas in her whole entire life and only fucked one, who was now the father of her two girls. She had been a virgin up until our senior year in high, but you know what they say opposites attract.

Tasha on the other hand had been my girl since 7th grade. We met at a dance audition at W.E. Greiner Exploratory Arts and Academy. Two peas in a pod we were. Standing at about five foot six, one hundred-twenty-three pounds of slimness and caramel complexion, she drove the niggas crazy with her stiffness. Mother of two boys and independent by any means necessary. Tasha was my go and get it bitch she wasn't taking no for an answer and I loved that about her.

We all went well together and anytime we linked it there was hell to pay on every level.

"Cammy Pooh, we are about to board the plane now." Tae screamed into the phone. It was always hard being away from my best friend and god daughter but college was a must. So every time we linked up it was a celebration. Luckily if everything went well their flight would only be one hour max. It was 9:30 A.M. so I had time to do come last minute shopping before having to pick them up.

"Ok, call me when you land, I'll be waiting in the lobby." I replied

"Oh and for the record, Asia backed out." She said nonchalantly.

That was no surprise to me as Asia was always the one to not follow through with the plans, even though they were planned months in advance. Either way we would still have fun with or without her.

"Lol, of course." I laughed into the phone.

"I'll see you and Tasha when you land."

"Love you, later baby." Tae said before hanging up the phone.

It would only take a few minutes for me to make it to William P. Hobby Airport, but I definitely didn't want to keep my girls waiting so my next stop after the Houston Galleria was straight to them.

Slim: "Where you at?"

Me: "I'm driving, where are you?"

Slim: "About to pull up at you crib."

Me: "I'll be there in a few, I had to make a few runs before we head out."

Slim: "Touché', you gone give me that pussy before you leave."

Me: "Maybe lol, maybe not."

Me: "But you know texting and driving is a no go, give me a second."

Slim: "Bet, I'll be here."

Slim: "You know you want me to kiss on it."

He must've been in a good mood and had forgotten about that fist fight we had just the other night when I noticed a hickie on his neck that I hadn't put there. On that day, Slim was the least of my concerns. I was headed to the airport to get my girls and it was only right I rolled my windows down and smoked some exotic Kush on the way.

"Look hop in my ride
Stash this,
Hold that,
Be cool turn
The sound up and roll that
Now you my gutta bitch"

"Gutta Bitch" by Webbie interrupted my music being played from my phone being it was plugged into the car by the auxiliary cord.

"Cammy Pooh." Tae's voice called.

"I'll be there in five minutes." I replied trying to hold back my laugh.

"Bitch your ass is never late, we just made it from getting our bags checked." She said.

"Hurry, up." She demanded.

I swear it was like a scene in a movie when I pulled up. Without even calling them to let them know I had arrived at the airport. I parked, popped the truck and yelled their names from across the way.

"Taeeeee."

"Tashaaaaa." I screamed.

Empress Hyder

You should've seen the looks on the white people's faces. "Did we give a damn?" Of course not, what was understood did not have to be explained.

After helping them get their things packed away, we were headed back to my apartment for a pre-game session and to get some rest before heading out in the next hour or so.

"So Cammy do we get to meet Slim." Tae asked.

"Fuck slim! Does he have a brother?" Tasha whispered.

Without answering either one of their questions, I switched gears of the conversation.

"So how was the flight?" I asked curiously, being I had never rode a plane.

"Cam don't play, you are not slick." Tae added before opening up a bottle of peach Cîroc.

If anyone knew how to get the party started it was her and I was always down for drinks of whatever.

The trip back to Sage Rd was faster than usual. Traffic was never light in Houston, but neither of us were complaining. I knew the girls may have been tired and before we made a 10 hour drive to Destin, Florida, that was over 580 miles, I wanted to make sure we all were well-rested.

"Make yourselves at home." I said to Tae and Tasha As we entered my apartment.

Before approaching my bedroom door that was shut in front of me, I lit my favorite lavender candle that sat on my kitchen island. I shushed Tae and Tasha from the hallway and placed my ear to the door because I heard someone talking inside of my bedroom.

"So are you going to tell her, or you want me to tell her." A female's voice said loud and clear. Not realizing how thin my doors and walls were I gave the conversation another two minutes. The voice was familiar but I wanted to be sure it was her especially since she was doing all the talking.

"If you won't I will. She needs to know." She replied.

Slim was usually soft spoken with a raspy voice so whatever he was saying she was responding to.

"Cammy." Tasha yelled from the living.

"Bitch the next time you have company take your sex tape out of the DVD player nasty." Tae added.

"Sex tape, what sex tape?" I replied, curious as to what they were talking about. Knowing they would have to come out of my room eventually I headed back towards to living room. Tae pressed play on the remote and instantaneously I could hear footsteps coming up the hallway.

"Well if that isn't you in the video Cammy, who is." Tasha and Tae asked.

The DVD had been sitting in my DVD player for weeks now and I had forgotten all about it. It was clear enough to make out Slim's tattoos, but I knew he wasn't dumb enough to have another bitch in my shit. Or maybe he was, because there was another bitch in my shit. In my room trying to get my nigga to tell me some shit he wasn't ready to tell me.

"Cam, if that isn't you....." we all paused as they both approached the living area shocked themselves to see that it was the two of them in the spotlight. Caught red handed, apparently on a camera that was probably set up for me.

The look on Slim's face was one I had never seen before. He was embarrassed. For the entirety of our existence, for one he looked concerned.

"Renay, so it's been you this whole time?" I asked as politely as I could as I stood up from where I was sitting.

"Camille, let me explain." She replied as Slim just stood silently.

"Renay?" Tae said as she walked to lock the door, because no one was leaving. Not even Slim.

"I think I'm going to just go." Renay retorted.

"Naw fam, ain't nobody going nowhere until you tell me what I need to be told." One thing for sure and two things for certain I was still from the grove, 65 that is and wasn't no bitch going to cross me. A side bitch had to be the saddest female known to mankind. *"Who could settle for being an option?"* Knowing you would never be someone's one and only so you slip up and get pregnant thinking you can keep a nigga. *"Who raised this bitch?"*

Everybody in the room knew they had better been glad that I was loaded. I really wasn't for my high being blown but my girls were ready to tussle.

"What kind of hoe are you to bite the hand that has fed you when you didn't have shit." I voiced waiting on a response.

"Hello." Confirming she knew who I was talking to.

I could see Tasha out the corner of my eye ready for war. She and Renay had a run-in back in the day so Tasha was waiting on the day to come face to face with her again. The vibe in the room had changed. The atmosphere was hostile. Slim was looking me dead in the face and hadn't said shit. Then again I wasn't trying to hear shit he had to say, that I hadn't heard before.

"Tell her." Renay shouted.

"Tell me what." I asked as I began to take steps in their directions. She knew I had a degree in whooping hoes in the street, so why would she cross me. I mean damn, the dick was good and maybe we had one too many conversations about how good it was. But this wasn't "Soul Food" and you weren't just about to fuck my nigga and think you could just leave. My hands were at her throat in the blink of an eye.

"TELL ME WHAT?" I repeated over and over again, but I guess if I would have let her go she could've responded.

"CJ Chill." Slim said grabbing my arms to release the grip I had on here.

"So, oh you gone save yo bitch....really....ok Slim, I see, I see." I replied pulling myself together. I readjust my clothes and took a step back to recollect my thoughts. And repeated, "Tell me what."

"Girl, are you pregnant or something?" Tae asked. "Tae chill, let the bitch answer the question." I declared. "Hello....man what do you have to tell me?"

"I'm here, right here in the flesh and now you're quiet."

Empress Hyder

"I'm pregnant," she whispered. You could hear the distress in her voice.

The rage started as a slow burning sensation in my chest and then it started growing like a volcano before it blows. This crumpling feeling took over my body. It was like being on your first roller coaster ride; everything was moving too fast to comprehend, and as you plunged down that steep hill your stomach lurches into your throat, choking you and making a huge tangle of your organs and intestines. And when the ride ends things are a bit clearer, but everything is still dizzy and you are a bit numb. Or, worse, all your nerves are alive as ever and your senses are heightened. But that wasn't the case. I wanted to get off this roller coaster. It was as if the whole world was spinning around fast but I was standing still. There were strings holding me down and everybody was watching me in the room, that one person out of the five of us who couldn't move.

"Get your shit and get out." I sniveled as I charged passed the both of them and headed towards my room. You would've thought we were in the Player's Club, when Diamond caught Ebony fucking Lance. But instead of letting the bitch hide in the bathroom and knocking on the door with a loaded gun, I dropped the clip on mine. It was him or her, whoever I saw first when I returned to the living room if they were still there. If had a say so, one of them, hell the both of them, would leave out of here on a stretcher.

"Cammy No." Tae yelled, as Slim dropped to the floor and everything after that was a blur.

Chapter Eleven

Empress Hyder

"Who are you to judge the life I live?

I know I'm not perfect

-and I don't live to be-

but before you start pointing fingers...

make sure your hands are clean!"

— Bob Marley

After what happened my mom stopped speaking to me and would send Dookie and Napier into town to check on me every now and then. Our last conversation plays over in my mind when I want to pick up the phone and call her. But I'd grown tired of kissing her ass. Countless of times we would have the same conversation about the same thing. I get it. I got it. As my mother her job was to protect, but if I wanted to bump my head, just let me.

"Camille, you can be the light to those trapped in darkness. Do you not want more for yourself?
"So he isn't good enough, ma."
"I'm not saying he isn't good enough for someone else, but no he isn't good enough for my daughter.
"Me and your father worked hard to keep you out of the streets."
"Well, ma, we aren't like you and daddy. We are much better."
"Camille do you have any new love interest."
"No ma, why do you?"
"Because if you did you wouldn't spend so much time worried about some nigga who will only destroy you in the life. I've been done. I've been you before and baby I just want more for you. You're pretty. You're smart. Camille you just deserve better"

Empress Hyder

"Thanks ma, but when I need your advice I'll ask for it. Ma, I love you, never think I don't. But I'm not a little girl anymore."

"Camille, first allow yourself to heal or resurface from the tide of expectations. Never place too much emphasis on another being. In that case you are only setting yourself up for self-destruction. We often fall victimized to our own expectations. You are a pure breed red nose like your father, going hard and determined to win, which is the proper attitude and perfect stance to have in today's generation."

"I love you ma."

"Camille, you are a trophy to any man, anywhere, whether he be the president, pope or a peasant. You are a true gift from God and an Angel here on earth to be the light to whoever needs your beckon to brighten their gloomy journey in life."

IT WAS SEPTEMBER 26TH and I seriously did not know how I made it through the end of last semester and the summer for that matter with all the bullshit that had went down. On a bad note Slim was still in the hospital recovering from my gunshot wound. The doctors at Westside Surgical Hospital said it would take anywhere from a three month to nine months for Slim to completely heal and become mobile again. The bullet went through his stomach and out his back missing his major arteries. Had it ruptured any of his stomach or any other organ he would have been dead in a matter of 15 minutes but God was not done with him yet and neither was I. Finally, Lamar and I were back on speaking terms. Tasha and Tae relocated to

Houston so that I could have a sense of home here with me until I graduated and Renay, well let's just say she's no longer with child.

Rook and I grew closer than ever.

While his brother was recovering, he was letting the neighbors know I knew his name. We had an empire to hold down. Slim put Rook in charge, I made most of the runs if not all and then we would spend most nights together three blocks away from my condo. His visits would become more frequent and it was only a matter of time we became inseparable.

I had dozed off into a nap when I got a phone call from Rook.

"Can I, can I save you from you
'Cause you know there's something missing
And that champagne you've been sippin's
Not supposed to make you different all the time
It's starting to feel like the wrong thing to do girl
'Cause with all that recognition it gets hard for you to listen"

"Hi baby."

"Open the door." He whispered into the phone, like someone was listening.

"It's open." I replied, knowing he was coming I had already unlocked the door so that I would not have to get up off the couch to let him in.

"That was fast." I said. It literally took him less than ten minutes to make it from the store and back.

"You missed me huh." He laughed.

"Maybe." I replied as he leaned in to give me a kiss on the forehead.

Empress Hyder

Rook was not your average prince charming he was far more suave than that. He was a killer with a baby face wasn't no denying that. At six foot two, one-hundred-eighty-six pounds of perfection, he was a Puerto Rican king. His skin was soft to the touch. He was not your average mixed-breed. He had a perfect set of teeth and a smile that was too die for. Those hazel eyes were piercing. When he looked in your direction you could tell they not only saw your body, your flesh but could read your soul. He was a little over four months older than me with no kids to his name. His body, lord that body, was drenched in tattoos, from head to toe. Perfectly fit and firm. He kept a fade so that his waves could breathe and two slits in each eyebrow. His cologne was as strong as midnight sex and just one sniff of it would have you hooked. He was a Leo so he was very confident and independent, and when it came to the business he was in command and in control. Deep inside he was sensitive but it was hidden very well. He needed to be needed and I wanted to be loved. I didn't know how I was going to juggle three niggas at one time but I was up for the test.

"Damn girl, it smells good in here." He said sniffing into the air interrupting our moment.

It was Sunday so it was only right I slow cooked a pot roast with potatoes and carrots in my crockpot Ruth had given me as a house warming gift. I had some turnip greens cooking on the back burner. Some jiffy cornbread with the sugar added baking on the bottom rack of the stove and his favorite brownies cooling on the counter by the refrigerator. I wasn't a Kool-Aid drinker but I had the ingredients on the counter waiting on him to get here so he could mix up his favorite diabetes in a cup.

As always he would setup shop so we could discuss what routes needed to be ran and what funds needed to be collected.

We were only a minute into our Sunday meeting when three knocks hit the front door.

Knock. Knock. Knock.

"Here we go again." I thought to myself.

"Who is it?" Rook yelled from the couch as he began to stuff his scale, cash and drugs ranging from marijuana to crack cocaine back into his duffle bag.

"Open the door." A deep voice said.

"Yeah, open up the door." Another voice said.
I knew those voices from anywhere, I took off to the door like I was running the 100 meter dash back in middle school.

"Dookie….Napier." I shouted, almost in tears. It had been almost a month since I'd seen my brothers and I missed my big niggas daily.

"What's up baby girl?" Dookie said as he began to bear hug me.

"What chu cooking?" Napier asked

They both paused and looked at each other, "I guess we are right on time." Dookie added.

"Rook what's up my boy." Napier stated as he approached the couch to dap Rook's hand.

"It ain't nothing, what chu boys been up to." Rook responded.

"Living trying to get in on this action." Dookie interrupted.

Empress Hyder

Dookie and Rook had been locked up together a few years ago. So they knew each other very well. They knew I was down with Slim and his squad but didn't really know how deep so visiting was all they were doing.

"The food is ready." I shouted from the kitchen.

"Well fix a nigga a plate or something." They all shouted back in unison.

Let Dookie tell it, bitches belonged in the kitchen barefoot and pregnant catering to her nigga.

Moment of honesty
Someone's gotta take the lead tonight
Whose it gonna be?
I'm gonna sit right here
And tell you all that comes to me
If you have something to say
You should say it right now
(Drake: You should say it right now)

I could hear my phone ringing from arm of the couch. I excused myself knowing it was Lamar and to avoid any problems it was best I spoke with him in the presence of no one.

"Hello." I said lowly, hoping no one was listening.

"What's up baby? Is everything alright?" Lamar asked.

"Everything is fine, Lamar." I replied

"Why would you ask something like that?" I had no clue what Lamar was talking about.

"Renay told me…." I paused him before he could finish.

"I don't give a fuck what Renay told you. Better yet, if you talking to the hoe, you're no better than him." I screamed into the phone before disconnecting the line. Unsure as to why he was still speaking to Renay. I made sure to call her over and over again but my calls would not go through. *"What the fuck had Renay told him and I hadn't spoken to that bitch in months?"*

Hadn't seen here around campus. Went to her momma house and she was not there. So as far as I was concerned she was dead to me.

I returned to what I was doing as if that phone call never happened. The boys were in the living room chopping it up as usual. I was putting something in my stomach before I ran some errands because I had at least 12 grand to collect from a few of our workers and some packages to drop off. Time waited for no one so I had to get moving.

"Anything else before I head out." I asked out loud. Rook began to write something on a piece of paper and told me to make sure that was my last stop for the night.

"Lock up my shit when ya'll leave." I said as I headed towards the elevator.

Chapter Twelve

"You can deceive yourself with truth too. That's an even more dangerous dream."

— Erich Maria Remarque

Empress Hyder

◆ ◆ ◆

My routine trips to our newest spot had been going well for the past three months. It wasn't until December 16th, the weekend before my 21st birthday that I would reach the spot and it was a madhouse. There was a lot of activity in the area being it was always my last stop and I would usually reach my final destination at about 8:30 P.M. The spot was packed with dope fiends. Regular and some new. Judging from the traffic flowing in and out of the house, we were probably making between eight to twelve grand a day, and that was on the low end. It was the first of the month so typically we would see an increase in new faces. Profit would triple around this time throughout the year. So it was only right to collect to prevent niggas from lying about how much they made. Some of our workers were honest and some were greedy. I sometimes hated making these runs alone but they knew who and who not to cross.

The niggas who ran this particular spot were some young Houston niggas, ages 18 and 20, the homeboys of one of one of Slim's baby mommas. Dee and Dre were their names. They stayed high from the looks of it and getting high off of my supply was definitely a violation.

Approaching the front door, I could see a car creeping out of my peripheral view. A blacked out impala, similar to the one that had been following me, for what seemed to be months now. Without making it obvious I slightly looked over my shoulder, with my hand on my strap as I knocked on the door. The fiends knew to ring the bell around back. So therefore if anyone knocked on the front door it had to be the laws or a boss. Our signature knock would tell the difference.

I couldn't name a nigga on the face of this earth who was stupid enough to run up in Slim's shit and rob his workers. No one would get away with it even if they had tried.

"Who is it?" Dee yelled from inside over the loud ass noise coming from the television. Without saying a word, I knocked again. A fiend hopped out of the impala that was now parked three house down and approached the porch and as soon as Dee opened the door to let me in, I was bum rushed with a gun cocked to my head.

"What the fuck is this?" I asked trying to remain calm.

"Shut the fuck up." The gunman said.

Almost simultaneously, two more niggas kicked in the back. The watch guy in the front tried to draw his pistol but he was too slow. I had been rushed so hard my .38 revolver slid under the couch.

"I'll give you anything you want if you let me go." I screamed.

Dee had been hit across the head with the butt of one the guys nine and had fallen to the floor, unconscious. Dre heard the commotion and ran towards the kitchen with his pistol drawn. He was in the back room bagging pills and counting money. When he came out the room he blindly fired several shots into the living room area, but none connected with the intended targets. I was lucky to avoid

Empress Hyder

not getting hit or grazed by all of the bullets that flew past me.

The gun man still had a gun drawn to my head as he drug me by my hair to a back room. He knew the layout all too well for this to be a random robbery.

"Who sent you my nigga?" I asked, screaming and kicking.

"Cesar, get the rope and shit so we can tie this bitch up, then we can blast these fools and get rid of the bodies." Cass said before removing the ski mask from over his face.

"Caesar?"

"Cass?"

I just knew they weren't the niggas behind this. Cursing under my breathe knowing they wouldn't get away with shit, I attempted to fight back while reaching for my cell phone to either call Slim or Rook to let them know their boy was tripping.

"Can I, can I save you from you
'Cause you know there's something missing
And that champagne you've been sippin's
Not supposed to make you different all the time
It's starting to feel like the wrong thing to do girl
'Cause with all that recognition it gets hard for you to listen
To the things that I must say to make you mine
But live girl, have some fun girl, we'll be fine
Trying to convince myself I've found one
Making the mistake I never learned from"

Rook was calling but I was unable to move because of the restraints Cass had on my arms. He had his knee in my back and my body pushed down into the floor applying all of his weight. All I could do was wait helplessly for Caesar to bring in the rope.

"I know you." I said to Caesar making sure to look him dead in his face as he entered the room.

"Shut this bitch up." He told the gun man as he began to reach around my pockets searching for my phone.

"I'll take that." Someone said coming into the room.

Relieved to hear his voice, I knew someone would come and save me. But the chances of that happening were rare. To my surprise that wasn't what he was there for.

"Maybe next time you'll think again before crossing me to fuck with my own flesh and blood." Slim said furiously. Before throwing my phone into the wall right above my head shattering the screen.

"You set this shit up." I screamed.

"What type of nigga are you, I'm a female." I added.

"Nah, you're a low-down filthy bitch Camille, ain't no coming back from that." Slim replied.

Once I was bound and tied up, Cass carried me over his shoulder to the only room in the house with a bed. I tried to wipe away the tears from my eyes with my shoulder. But no matter what took place I knew justice would be served. I mean I knew Slim would retaliate. I just didn't know how and when.

I wonder if Rook was in on this. Don't you dare cry Camille. Karma is a motherfucker and they would get theirs. You are much stronger than this. No weapon formed against you will prosper. Get it together. It is only a matter of time before someone shows up.

Empress Hyder

I dapped the corner of my eyes with the fabric from my tee shirt. And tuned out everything in the room that was being done. There were needles being shot into my veins. My body began to feel numb. Caesar was in the corner snorting lines. And from the looks of it I could tell these niggas had a hidden agenda.

Cass flipped my limp body around on the bed and began to tug at my pants. Caesar decided he wanted to help after feeding his nostrils, so he gripped me by the hair and sloppily kissed my lips down to my neck. They tore my blouse off of my body and had their way with me.

I could feel Cass struggling before Caesar pushed him out of the way.

"Let me go first." He said excitedly.

"What was the shit you were talking that day at your crib." He said with anger before ramming his dick into my dry pussy.

"Caesar stop." I screamed while trying to get him off of me.

"Caesar please stop." I pleaded.

"Shut up." Yelled Cass as he began inserting his dick into my mouth. Subconsciously I wanted to bite his shit off but he still had his pistol near. I was gagged, gang raped and doped up all at the same time and no one was around to help me. I laid there damn near lifeless, but aware enough to hear the door open. I swear it was like a fucking rodeo.

"What the fuck is going on in here." Slim asked.

"Just having a little fun." Caesar replied.

"A little too much fun." Slim said and before I could cry out to him, shots were fired and the weight on Caesar's body collapsed on top of me.

"Oh my god.....oh my god, Slim what did you do?" I cried out frantically. I could feel the warmth of his blood seeping onto my back as he gasped for his last breathe.

"Fuckkkkk......what the fuck." I screamed.

"Slim help me please....baby, please, I'm sorry." I pleaded

Although he never spoke a word, I could see Lucifer himself in his eyes, he returned to embrace me, giving me a ray of hope that maybe we were even.

"Baby, I'm sorry, I promise I'll make it up to you." I cried. Ignoring me, he untied my arms and freed my legs and stared at me in digest. My body was weak so I struggled to get my clothing back intact. Offering no help at all he left me where I sat, in a room where two dead bodies lied. *"Why would you murder the niggas you sent to set me up in cold blood?"*

Nothing was adding up. Not one thing from that night made sense.

I was still feeling a little woozy, I could barely feel my legs and my vision was a tad bit blurry. I could hear the sirens from police cars, an ambulance and a firetruck. Someone had called 911, and I had to flee the scene before any charges got pinned on me.

SOME PRE-BIRTHDAY CELEBRATION.

Chapter Thirteen

"I will no longer mutilate and destroy myself in order to find a secret behind the ruins."

— Hermann Hesse

Empress Hyder

◇ ◇ ◇

It was early on a Wednesday morning and a month before graduation and I was moving slowly around my apartment. I had just been released from the hospital after being diagnosed with HIV.

Lamar, Tasha and Tae had all stopped by before I headed out to pick up Rook from the Federal State Penitentiary. He caught a felony drug charge the night after Slim left the scene from the trap. In addition to the thousands of dollar in fines we had to pay he was sentenced to a little under a year.

Slim and I were no longer on speaking terms, other than the two or three times we had sex for old time sakes. He was good for something but after the shit he pulled I decided that pawning my engagement ring was the best way to prove that we were officially over.

Ring. Ring

I jumped with excitement at the ring of my phone.

"You have a collect call from…..Rook." The operator said.

"Baby." The sound of his voice came through the phone and my heart began to flutter.

"Hello……Rook….I miss you." I said.

"I miss you too! I just wanted to hear your voice, we made it to Huntsville, and I'm on my way to Houston….meet me downtown." He replied.

I missed Rook badly and those past couple of months had been tough. Gladly he would be home right before the Thanksgiving holiday. Dookie and Napier would be coming into town but my mom was stuck on me coming to Dallas. I was losing my balance and needed gravity to stay the hell away for me. I became irritated by the back and forth madness between myself and this love triangle. Every time I would get off of good terms with one the others would get in where they thought they could fit in. Every time I would come from visiting Rook we would always be in a good place so I would always regret the damage I had done to myself and him unknowingly. There was love and lust flying all over the place, however something was continuously holding on to Lamar, and that something had to be love. *"Only once in your life, I truly believe, you find someone who can completely turn your world around. You tell them things that you've never shared with another soul and they absorb everything you say and actually want to hear more. You share hopes for the future, dreams that will never come true, goals that were never achieved and the many disappointments life has thrown at you..."* Bob Marley wrote.

Love, that kind of love, would trick you into staying and being miserable in fear of starting over. And starting over was something I just couldn't see myself doing. I knew deep down inside my heart Lamar would win when it was all said and done. But I too deserved to have some fun. I didn't want to feel like I had wasted all those year. I was praying that things would change and he would at least put forth the same effort he did when it came to football and hustling to

Empress Hyder

make ends meet to pay all those damn doctor bills his moms was racking up. At this point Rook would be my go to nigga, nothing more and nothing else, and I knew he would understand.

"What did I really want?"
"What did I really need?"
"Who was I doing this for?"
"Was I supposed to change?"
"Who would really be the one for me?"

As I made that ten minute drive through those Houston city streets, questions began tautening my mind.

I could see the bus approaching its stop in my rear view mirror. The excitement that took over my body was intense, but I tried to keep my composure.

"So what's all that talk about missing me?" I heard a voice say before entering the car.

"Well we meet again." I said trying to stop myself from blushing.

He reached over and gave me a hug signifying he never wanted to let me go. For about five minutes we sat in the same spot and enjoyed each other's company with no restrictions.

"You know it's about to go down." He said as usually. "I'm more ready than ever." I replied staring at him as I pulled off into a howling full moon.

Me: "We are headed back, is Lamar still there?"
Tae: "He's gone."
Tasha: "Bitch, I'm sick of your shit, lol."
Me: "Lol, ok."

Me: Ya'll can go home now damn, I'll see ya'll tomorrow.

Tae: "Damnnnnn"

Tasha: "Girl, I ain't made at you."

Me: "Bye, ayeeeee, clean up my shit."

We barely made it to the parking garage, yet along my apartment before I climbed in the back seat and welcomed him to join me.

"Come on." I said with a slight head nod directing him to the back seat of the car. Luckily my windows were tinted and if they weren't anyone in the parking garage would have just had to witness some public affection.

"That's how you want?" He asked.

"Come on." I repeated.

My panties were off and my legs were wide open and the look on his face was priceless. Usually we would use condoms but I wasn't stopping and looking for one was not happening. He had some pressure built up and even the scent of a women would called his dick to rupture. Everything about sex in a car was exciting. Even more exciting when the sex was better than love. Once he got in his zone, he dived right in, head first.

"ohhh, baby you eat this pussy so good." I moaned as I gripped the crown of his head. My legs were touching both sides of the car and my eyes were rolling into the back of my head.

I knew then he wanted me wet enough to where it felt like he was drowning, but I wanted to be in charge and wanted him to relax and not work too hard and work up a sweat.

Empress Hyder

"Damn, baby you taste as good as I remember." He said with a mouth full of my juices as he looked me in my eyes. Like he brother, it felt like he was penetrating my soul.

"Put it in." I demanded reaching to assist him in unzipping his pants. With ease his dick was in his right hand, his left hand was pulling my body closer to him. He tugged at my shirt for it to come off so that he could lick my nipples, because he knew that was my spot. He slid two fingers into me as he glided his dick into my pussy.

"Ooooooo.....shit," I whimpered, by that time I could feel my clitoris throbbing. I probably had nutted about two times already and we had just started.

"Damn baby, your shit is wet." He moaned.

I swear, that was the best hour of my life, enjoying the sounds of love making as, "Is it the way," by Jill Scott played in the background.

"Is it the way you love me baby?"
"Is it the way you love me baby?"

The lyrics to the song faded into the rhythm of the night as our bodies came together in harmony and once we were done we just laid there.

Laid in the puddles formed from our lust; satisfied.

July 9th, 2015

Empress Hyder

"If people refuse to look at you in a new light and they can only see you for what you were, only see you for the mistakes you've made, if they don't realize that you are not your mistakes, then they have to go."

— Steve Maraboli

◆ ◆ ◆

At 9:38 P.M. and 9:42 P.M. I gave birth to my baby girls. Baby A was 4 pounds 5 ounces and Baby B was 5 pounds 7 ounces. The love that overcame me was one I had never known.

My water didn't break as most women would describe, it had to be broken for me which really brought on the contractions. I had now dilated to 9 centimeters and my bags were bulging. Dr. Reddy called for an anesthesiologist for my epidural to relieve of the pain that came along with labor. My epidural began wearing off, my body was becoming chilled and I could feel myself getting sick. Labor was supposed to be excited and I was beyond frustrated. I think I was calling for the nurses every 5 minutes to get the show going.

"Miss Jones, Dr. Reddy has arrived." My charge nurse said peeping into my dimmed lite room before Dr. Reddy made his appearance.

About 10 minutes passed and I was become restless and not to mention I was starving because they wouldn't let me eat.

"We are going to monitor your contractions for a few minutes and then it will be show time." Dr. Reddy said after introducing himself to myself and my family. It was only a matter of second they would come back in the room, because I could feel pressure, a lot of pressure in my private area. I was beginning to crown. I had been in labor fifty-two hours before any action took place and it was finally time.

"Who would you like in the room with you?" The charge nursed asked. I had a room full of guest, but out of everyone only Tae and my mom would make the cut.

"Push." Tae and my mom screamed as they held my hand so that I could remain calm.

"Push." They repeated over and over again. After three big pushes and a few screams to relieve myself of the pain I pushed.

"There goes the head." Dr. Reddy responded as he pulled "Baby A- Laila Marie Jones" out.

It was time for me to push again, but I was ready to give up. My body felt as it did on the day Slim set me up.

"Miss Jones, you have to push." Dr. Reddy said calmly.

"I can't. I just can't." I cried.

"You can do it bestie." Tae chanted.

"There goes some hair." My mom cheered.

I remember myself screaming and crying and out she slid "Baby B- Kalie Danielle Jones". My body exhaled and it was over. They were finally here. The best thing out of this Dallas-Houston love triangle; my girls.

They would have to spend the next few days in neonatal care to get their jaundice level down being they were both born with bruises on their bodies. In the meantime, everyone wanted a paternity test to make sure at least one of them were the father. So I had that on my to-do list times three. The nurses were in and out my room drawing blood and checking on me. I just wanted to sleep but I wanted you guys to know I'm officially a new mother.

Overall, the experience has been life changing and altering at the same time. I'm exhausted. My mom has not left my side and to get my girls home faster I constantly have to carry them my breastmilk down to NICU. They told me I would be discharged by Sunday so the last steps were to go purchase a few at home DNA test so I could move the hell on with my life.

Lamar: "Are they here?"

Me: "Yes, you're about two hours late."

Lamar: "I'll be in town tomorrow with a test."

Me: "Ok, see you then.

My Facebook was blowing up with notifications from people congratulating me and welcoming me to mother hood.

Slim: "How much did they weigh?"

Me: "Laila Marie was 4 pounds 5 ounces and Kalie Danielle was 5 pounds 7 ounces"

Slim: "Damn, I hate I missed it, when are you going home?"

Me: "It's no big deal, and they said Sunday."

Slim: "Cool, I'll be back in town by then, can I come by?"

I could barely keep my eyes open and you won't believe who had just walked in when I began to doze off.

"How are you feeling?" Rook asked from behind the nurse who was coming in to refill my hospital cup with ice.

"Writing the end of our story." I replied.

Empress Hyder

"Congratulations…..congratulations on everything and I mean that." He said with that award winning smile.

After graduation, I packed my shit and moved back to Dallas. I left everything behind and during that transition Rook and I grew distant. He had moved on with some model chick he meet from Atlanta and gave up the drug game to go to school for welding. So to see him in Dallas, physically in front of me was a complete shocker.

"Thank you Rook, It's nice to see you." I replied as he leaned down to give me a hug.

But that was a few days ago. Currently I'm sitting here drinking a cup of sweet tea from Golden Chick, trying to calm my nerves. My mom called me to let me know the mail has arrived as I have been waiting on the results for all three potential fathers to find out who the father of the girls were.

Pacing back and forth, I called Tae to see if she would do me the honor of giving me the news so we could be done with it all.

Finally the wait was over and I'm feeling a little uneasy. The girls will be home tomorrow and the demons that have been haunting me would be laid to rest. I never thought over time I would lose myself, be mentally, physically, and sexually abused. Be betrayed by a bitch who I have given my last two. Be involved in a love triangle between the love of my life and two brothers. Be diagnosed with HIV all before finding out that I was pregnant on my 24th birthday and not know who the father is. That is what my life had become. My mother tried to warn me. She tried to protect me from this hurt but I'm taking full responsibility for my actions as a real woman would. I'm far from perfect and we all make mistakes. Hell as you've witnessed I made plenty.

With those mistakes I could either let my surrounding drown me out or use them as tools to make me better.

"Are you ready?" Tae asked.

"Of course I'm not ready to find out the truth, but I'm dying to get it over with." I replied.

We are down to the last envelope of results after two came back excluded.

"The alleged father is not excluded as the biological father of the tested child. Based on testing results obtained from analyses of the DNA loci listed, the probability of paternity is 99.99996%. The probability of paternity..." Tae paused.

And there it was, out of the three how I would tell Slim and Lamar they were not the father. Nevertheless, how would I call Rook and tell him, after so many years of being childless, he now had two.

Never in a million years could you have made me believe I would end up here again. In a place where I have felt unappreciated and striped of my self-confidence. I was supposed to be that bitch that no one could break. I was known for breaking hearts and getting what I wanted out of niggas with no feelings involved before meeting Lamar. I got myself here, so there was no one to be mad at or to blame but myself. My actions spoke for themselves and the consequences were coming in full effect. No regrets because once upon a time Lamar, Slim and Rook were exactly what I craved and I was willing to risk it all to maintain my position. A position when it was all said and done, I never had. Even if that meant going to war with the man I once loved and a bitch I once called my friend.

In the end, we all lost something. But I gained two of the greatest blessings any woman could ever ask for. It's kind of fucked up that I don't know how much longer I will have with them. Hopefully this HIV virus doesn't put me six feet under before I have a chance at rebirthing myself. We all deserve a second chance but being that this all was done in vain, I'm probably exempt.

Who knows where life will take me, when it was all and said and done. As long as I didn't go back to where life had took me then I might have something to look forward to.

Rook: "Slim has just be arrested."
Me: "For what?"
Rook: "The murder of Renay."

And that's how it all went down. That's my story, my truth. My past and the present. The Tell All of Camille Jones. I'm sure, sooner or later they will tell their side. We all know how the saying goes, there's three sides to every story, and on that note you have mine.

Until next time.

Signed, Camille Nadia Jones

To be continued in:

The Tell All of Camille Jones
Slim Unloaded

Empress Hyder

E Simone's Commentary

I hope that you enjoyed *The Tell All of Camille Jones* as much as I enjoyed writing it. It took me a little over a year to be exact to finally find the courage to tell her story. Not just her story but the story of many women who lose themselves in the situations we face throughout life. This story. Her story. My story evoked many emotions in me, and I gave much thought and allocated many long nights to constructing the characters and the overall story line. As women we must understand that we are worthy of being loved not because of what we have to offer between our legs but knowing love runs deeper than the pussy. From a male aspect, speaking on behalf of my male readers, you must understand that money is an accessory. It's nice to have, just like nice cars and nice clothes. But if that's all you have to offer than no woman you come in contact with will last.

    Camille had the best of both worlds some people would think, when Slim and Lamar were very similar in almost everything. Their upbringing from the hood, their love for football, and the love they both shared for Camille. Different in the paths they decided to take but that was it. Every character in this story loved hard and yearned to be loved. They all just carried it out in their actions differently. Some needed it more than other but were too prideful to let it flow and I've come to realize that a lot of people are exactly like this. Will go to the extreme to hurt someone and make them feel so high and so low all at the same time, to satisfy their own personal needs.

There are so many lessons to learn from in this story and stories to come. In this book, I wanted to show you how temptation can creep up on you and change your life in a matter of minutes. This storyline is a prime example of how a simple conversation could lead to something unintended.

Camille's relationship with Lamar, Slim and even Rook brought her down in so many ways. Her self-esteem and confidence were ripped from her, causing her to bury her insecurities in the sheets of many unknown men.

I encourage you to want more for yourself than settling for temporary happiness. Women and men, we should never sacrifice our own happiness for material things or other people, period. I don't care who you are, where you've came from or how you turned out, everyone is entitled to happiness. While many people come in our lives expectantly, remembering not all of them are meant to stay can be a hard pill to swallow.

Empress Hyder

Toxic relationships are unhealthy for everyone involved. You must release the toxic and infectious relationships, friendships and even jobs, and take back your time and your heart. Karen Salmansohn once said, "Sometimes it's better to end something and try to start something new than imprison yourself in hoping for the impossible."

Overall, the experience of completing my first book has been an emotional rollercoaster. The completion of this book was kind of like birthing your first child. Not only did I create a character to take on some important events that happened in my life but I've helped tell the story of many readers who can relate. This experience has been life-changing. Thank you for reading!

Love and Light,

E' Simone

The Reader's Corner

This section is dedicated to all of my supporters who've sent emails, left encouraging comments and followed my blog at empressu4what.blogspot.com from the very beginning. Over 17 thousand views, it would have been impossible without any of you. "Nmm,ffffffffffff gcd dv 9 kk   I dfzvc" (From Zyion to my readers)

C. Smith wrote: "Let me tell you something. You fucking did that. If this didn't give me flashbacks on some of my own skeletons. Yaaassssss, love, love….loved it. People need to pay for this."
E. Blakemore wrote: "I swear I can't help but read your book and just visualize and think back to our college days."
Y. Williams wrote: "I'm not one to predict what will happen in the future but I know part 70-75 is finna be amazing."
N.Smith wrote: "I have officially made MsEmpress blog a favorite to read and get the tea every day. The Tell All of Camille Jones…you guys have to tune in."
T. Gabriel wrote: "I just got done diving into this blog by my college roomie MsEmpress #empressu4what #jobwelldone #keepitup love ya chick."
E.Lashay wrote: "I'm getting my copy, I'll be the first one in line."
C. Ross wrote: "This is good!!!!"
S. Brown wrote: "Omgod give me more!! I need this book. I check your page everyday time I log on!!!"

Empress Hyder

S. Jones wrote: "My baby has the gift. I'm ridiculously proud of you! I cannot wait to get my signed autographed copy."

J. Carter wrote: "Another proud big sister moment….my little sister has done it again, she's an awesome writer. If you haven't read it, you need to…"

A. Leake wrote: "This is my first time I actually read something from your book other than the title. Now that I got all into it…You stop. Like that's all I get! Ok I'm ready for the book. I was buying it anyway but now you got me wondering what happens next. Like I really need to know…Good Job."

D. Tatum wrote: "Hot Damn, I'm ready!"

S. White wrote: "Omg!! Come on December damn..!! Go Emp.!!!"

J. Coleman wrote: "Calling all readers and writers, support the talented young woman MsEmpress and her blog empressu4what.blogspot.com."

Q. Watson wrote: "Kind of gotten glued to your blog and I must say it's definitely interesting…"

L. Fantroy wrote: "Girl I'm hooked, I love it."

T. Bell wrote: "Started reading "The Tell All of Camille Jones," last Saturday and ending up finishing part 1-54 in a few hours….I will need a copy officially signed by you. Thanks."

T. Burks wrote: "Hey, so I just sat in my room and read your entire blog….I couldn't take my eyes off the screen…You're truly talented."

S. Lawrence wrote: "Man maybe I haven't been reading books lately, but this is some of the best/only shit I've read. You have my attention. Good shit."

R. Strogen wrote: "Girl, I like this, is this her real life story! It's good though and I'm tuned in foreal."
Fancy Nancy wrote: "Some trill shit."
J. Dillard wrote: "I just read all of "The Tell All of Camille Jones." You are a wonderful writer. I usually don't read books or blogs like this but you made read through everything in one night. It was that good. Keep going.........You are well on your way in the writing arena!"
B. Shardai wrote: "Very well written!! You have me on the edge and ready to continue reading to see what is next!!! I am proud of you keep up the great work."
S. Taylor wrote: Girl yes, I'm hooked! Can't wait for the next part. And I got my coworkers on to your blog too! They all said, "Girl this is good." Keep writing and stay blessed.
C. Bufford wrote: "I just started reading on Saturday and I couldn't stop reading now I'm **hooked....**"
J. Fields wrote: "The entry leaves me wanted to know what happens next."
J. Crawford wrote: "Can't wait to read what you have next to come."
E. Brown wrote: "What's next? Ready for the book. Thank you for sharing your talent."
Chynadoll wrote: "If you haven't captured all my attention. You go girl!"
Anonymous 1 wrote: "I just started reading, great job, I'm glued."
Anonymous 2 wrote: "I just wanted to say your blogs are amazing. I just read every single last one of them and you are such a strong person to share your story with

everybody...keep striving, you're definitely on the road to success."

Anonymous 3 wrote: "For those who read and find this even a tad bit interesting needs to follow @empressu4what for more of this juicy story. You have a gift and Thanks for sharing...."

Anonymous 4 wrote: "Freaking awesome"

Anonymous 5 wrote: "I just read all of your blogs since day one! It took about 2 hours. You are a courageous person to put your life on display for the world to judge...your life is an amazing story...Keep up the great work!"

Anonymous 6 wrote: "You have me on the edge of my seat. Keep'em coming."

Anonymous 7 wrote: "Wow! I love your writing."

Empress Hyder